Drama Workshops for Anger Management and Offending Behaviour

Drama Workshops for Anger Management and Offending Behaviour

James Thompson

Jessica Kingsley Publishers
London and Philadelphia

First published in the United Kingdom in 1999 by
Jessica Kingsley Publishers Ltd,
116 Pentonville Road, London
N1 9JB, England
and
325 Chestnut Street,
Philadelphia PA 19106, USA.

www.jkp.com

© Copyright 1999 James Thompson

Library of Congress Cataloging in Publication Data
Thompson, James, 1966–
Drama workshops for anger management and offending behavior /
James Thompson.
p.   cm.
Includes bibliographical references and index.
ISBN 1 85302 702 2 (pbk. : alk. paper)
1. Psychodrama. 2. Anger. 3. Aggressiveness (Psychology) I. Title
RC489.P7T524   1999
616.89'1523--dc21   98--42743 CIP

British Library Cataloguing in Publication Data
Thompson, James
Drama workshops for anger management and offending behaviour 1. Prison theatre
2. Drama – Therapeutic use
I. Title
365.6'6

ISBN 1 85302 702 2

Printed and Bound in Great Britain by
Athenaeum Press, Gateshead, Tyne and Wear

CONTENTS

Acknowledgements	7
Introduction	9
The programme and the workshop	39

BLAGG! – THE HISTORY	40

THE BLAGG! MANUAL	46
Introduction	46
Type and size of group	46
Space and the set	47
Timings	48
Using the manual	49
The exercises	49
Starting off	49
Describing Blagg!	49
Part 1	50
1 Warm-ups	50
2 How to play	53
3 Who is Jo Blaggs?	60
4 What has s/he done?	62
5 What is Jo thinking?	63
6 Who is affected?	65
7 Consequence pictures	69
8 Activating the image	71
9 Jo's new thoughts and feelings	74
Part 2	75
1 Why did it all happen?	75
2 The escape	79
3 Deroling	82

Further development   84

    1 Following on   84

    2 Repeat Blagg!   85

    3 Blagg! with a real 'Jo'   85

    4 Beliefs   85

    5 Social skills   86

    6 Decisions and consequences   86

    7 Alternative Blagg!   86

    8 Video   87

The end?   87

PUMP! – THE HISTORY   88

THE PUMP! MANUAL   93

Introduction   93

Type and size of group   93

Space   94

Timings   95

Describing Pump!   95

The course aims and objectives   95

The sessions   96

    1 The Pump!   96

    2 Deflating the Pump!   106

    3 Deflating the Pump! (2)   111

    4 Jack!   116

    5 Jacks out!   122

    6 The behaviour box (1)   125

    7 The behaviour box (2)   130

    8 Feedback, evaluation and the future   135

Appendices

    1 Model diary   139

    2 Knocks, Wind-Ups and Pumps guide   140

References   141

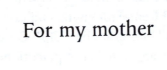

For my mother

Acknowledgements

I would like to thank all at the TIPP Centre past and present for support and guidance in writing this edition. They are Michael Balfour, Jacqui Burford, Rowan Davies, Bridget Eadie, Paul Heritage, Tom Hogan, Kate Lodge, Nic Nuttgens, Amie Proudman, Louis Reynolds, Simon Ruding, Anna Sevink, and Melanie Thomas. A special thank you to Jocelyn Meall whose ingenuity and stunning design contributed hugely to the development of both the projects. I would also like to thank the staff at Manchester University Drama Department and the board of the TIPP Centre for giving endless time and support. Credit for this book goes to all those at the TIPP Centre, Greater Manchester Probation Service and the large number of practitioners and participants who were involved in the devising of these projects. A particular mention should go to Ali Campbell for inspiring several of the exercises. Another thanks must go to Bev Rowson who had faith to commission the Blagg! workshop in the first instance and to Anne Power who continued the invaluable commitment of Greater Manchester Probation Service to this work.

A final thank you goes to Debbie for allowing me to retreat to the attic so often, and Hannah and Leah who were always there to make sure I came back down again.

James Thompson

Introduction

This book is about practice that sits across two separate disciplines. The Blagg! Offending Behaviour Workshop and the Pump! Anger Management Programme are examples of both applied theatre and therapeutic groupwork programmes. They exist as examples of cross-disciplinary work, illustrating how the creative arts can interact with an area of social policy. In addition, they demonstrate how each of these fields can extend the remit of the other. They do not only show how two forms of practice can 'meet in the middle', but how each provide a framework through which to view and perhaps offer a critique of the other. It has been noted by the theatre researcher Marvin Carlson, in comparing how performance theory has engaged with many areas of the social sciences, that 'the strategies and the theories of the behavior therapists have attracted…less attention from theatre theorists' (Carlson 1996, p.47). This edition, in a small way, rises to this challenge by examining these fields in a theoretical framework, as well as providing guidelines to practice in the form of manuals.

Before discussing the history and genesis of the Blagg! Workshop and the Pump! Programme in detail, this introduction will examine the two fields and provide an outline of how they meet and complement one another in a dynamic way. The aim is to provide a brief overview of the current movement to support offender rehabilitation programmes and also to suggest spheres where theatre and drama may interact with this growing field.

APPLIED THEATRE

This book is, on the one hand, about applied theatre. That is, theatre removed from a traditional (perhaps building-based) context and applied to the objectives of wider social institutions, organisations and agencies. The term 'theatre' is used to include all those processes, techniques, approaches and skills that are in any way components of drama practice. This may be scripted performance, participatory workshops, a single moment of role play, or an extended rehearsal sequence. It may include the performance of Shakespeare in a secure hospital (Cox 1992), psychodrama with capital offenders (Thompson

1998b), or forum theatre with slum dwellers in Rio De Janeiro (Boal 1998). In applying these techniques to what are broadly known as areas of social policy, practitioners are concerned to realise both the obvious and perhaps hidden potential of theatrical practice in meeting different needs.

In 'meeting the needs' it is important to note that theatre does not become a subsumed practice in these contexts. Theatre approaches interact with an agency's objectives, sometimes to fulfil them, sometimes to extend them and occasionally to undermine them. Theatre's contact is with the audience or participants first, and the social institution second. Sometimes that institution has a contradictory relationship with these people (the prison that seeks to rehabilitate and punish) and sometimes is grows from the participants and is controlled by them (see the Movimento Sem Terra in Brazil)[1]. The application of theatre may fit snugly or it may grate, it may become an easy complement or a point of friction. An extended use of creative role play in the classroom may be rewarding for the young people, but come into conflict with the tight objectives of a pre-set curriculum. A play on a hospital ward might relieve tension and anxiety amongst a group of patients but disrupt the routine of a consultant. Alternatively, the performance by a group of disabled young people might complement perfectly the work of the agency that seeks to promote their education and development. Theatre in an institution may be welcomed wholeheartedly by one section of staff but treated with suspicion by another. Theatre in a particular neighbourhood may galvanise a large section of the population transforming their expectations and opportunities (Heritage 1998). Theatre practice has appeared in health, education, criminal justice, 'third world' development and many other settings. Theatre 'works' in these areas, but in ways that are not simple or singular. Whilst there is often a need to define the specific functions – theatre developing personal self-confidence, or a community's ability to self-advocate for example – we should also understand that these separate functions are part of a complete process. Theatre is about the rehearsal and representation of the whole of human behaviour and experience.

Applying theatre is of course not a simple activity. The group of theatre practitioners who arrive at a prison gate and announce to the guards that they have come to undermine the institution are not going to do much theatre. Applied theatre practice must develop expertise in its area of application in order to get through any metaphorical gates. It requires not an invasion from the outside but a deep understanding of the arena in which you aim to work. Only with a clear understanding of another's objectives will theatre practice

[1]   The Movimento Sem Terra – the Landless People's Movement – is a landless labourers' movement in Brazil, campaigning for major agrarian reform.

find its place, where it can be effective and where it can complement, extend, and perhaps transform. The claim is made within these pages that offending behaviour groupwork and anger management use many theatre-based techniques and references. The work of an applied theatre practitioner can expand these moments, add a different insight to them and enrich the overall experience. The language of one form of practice (predominantly cognitive behavioural therapy in the case of the programmes outlined here) informs another (participatory drama work) and vice versa. The practice that emerges grows from these two sources. Probation officers might talk about Forum Theatre – group created scenes that present a commonly held problem in which the audience intervenes to rehearse solutions (see Boal 1992, pp.17–26) – as if it were a standard part of offender rehabilitation programmes. Theatre practitioners might refer to 'thinking errors' – where a person misinterprets reality, viewing their impression as objective fact rather than a subjective opinion – as if they had always been part of theatre workshop practice. At best this is not a process of mutual compromise but effective synthesis. Applied theatre at its best will aim for, what the educationalist Paulo Freire called, 'cultural synthesis'. Freire explained that:

> In cultural invasion, the actors draw the thematic content of their action
> from their own values and ideology; their starting point is their own world,
> from which they enter the world of those they invade. In cultural synthesis,
> the actors who come from 'another world' to the world of the people do so
> not as invaders. They do not come to *teach* or *transmit* or to *give* anything,
> but rather to learn, with the people, about the people's world. (Freire 1970,
> p.161)

The challenge for applied theatre practitioners is to offer the opportunity for this synthesis rather than to invade; to learn with people rather than teach. These are difficult objectives in any field, but they are particularly challenging in the world to which I will now turn.

OFFENDER REHABILITATION

This book is also about offender rehabilitation and groupwork. This section aims to give an overview of the field, how it has changed and how wider issues of crime policy impact directly on groupwork practice. It will start by setting the contextual scene and move on to where and how theatre can meet this area of practice. The drama workshops described later can only really be understood in the light of the sketch offered here.

WHAT WORKS?

'What works?' has been a rallying call for many areas of public policy and has in the last decade become the title of a series of conferences organised by Probation Services in the UK. These conferences have drawn together criminal justice researchers and practitioners from the US, UK and occasionally Europe. They have showcased innovative programmes, been the platform for outlining effectiveness criteria in criminal justice interventions, and sought to counter simplistic approaches to dealing with crime. They have been partly responsible for a major move towards developing 'evidence-based practice' (Chapman and Hough 1998) in probation in groupwork programme delivery. The publication of *Evidence Based Practice* represents the logical conclusion of this movement with formal government approval being given to the 'what works?' agenda.

It is important, however, to understand where the motivation for the question 'What works?' originated. The debate over rehabilitation of offenders has a major reference point in 1974 when the criminologist Martinson (1974) proclaimed after an exhaustive study of intervention programmes with offenders that 'nothing works'. Part of the recent history of the scholarly work in this debate (focused predominantly within the field of criminal psychology) has been one of either supporting or countering this standpoint. A number of the contributors to the 'What Works' conferences (see McGuire 1995) have spent many years working to refute its certainty. Even if this is to replace the 'nothing works' doctrine with the barely more optimistic 'almost nothing works' of Palmer (1996). It is a field where it seems some researchers *want* to believe something – to believe that there are intervention programmes that can effectively rehabilitate offenders (see Gendreau 1996) and others *want* to believe that Martinson was correct – that nothing works (Palmer 1996). Without entering the discussion as to the precise meaning of the word 'works', it is clear that this book sits within a continuing academic debate.

Before I go on to discuss the research work that was undertaken to dispute Martinson, it is important to examine briefly some of the effects of 'nothing works' on the development of the rehabilitation field. What the doctrine did was to place several frames around criminal justice practice and research, pushing the work in certain directions. One response was that the system's purpose became much more explicitly the management and punishment of offenders. It provided an impetus for an increase in the policy of 'just deserts', deterrence (Gendreau 1996, p.117), and for a political dichotomy between soft and hard on crime. If people were incorrigible, the only question remaining was how hard you punished them, and how to manage them whilst you were doing it. Although this soft/hard split has always been behind much of the popular discussion of crime (see for example, *The Times*, 12 June 1997), a climate where a newly endorsed 'nothing works' theory is coupled with a public demand for the politicians to 'do something' in reaction to a perceived rise in crime rates, means the debate becomes focused on these divisions even further. In other words, 'if you do this, you are soft', 'if you do that, you are hard'. Long prison sentences are hard and are therefore good. A theatre programme in the community is way down the soft line and is 'bad'. This was the difficult climate in which both the Pump! and the Blagg! programmes were created. Their existence is testimony to the belief that programmes and rehabilitative effort are valuable, but also they are evidence of the fact that policy making can never be the simple exercise of political will from the top down.

Michael Howard, the Home Secretary between 1993 and 1997 was famed for promoting the idea that 'prison works'. This was not necessarily because he thought it did, but may have been because he knew that this was 'hard' and therefore popularly equated with 'good sense'. His claim was, as stated by Harland in his discussion of US politicians and the crime issue, 'based more on hunch and ideology' (Harland 1996, p.75) than real understanding. It was of course a response that demonstrates his acceptance of the 'nothing (rehabilitative) works' position. Similar 'hunch and ideology' has informed much of the popular political debate in the US for several years. It has been one of the major stimuli to the expansion of prisons and the abandonment of rehabilitation initiatives (see Miller 1996). In this context, rehabilitation has not only been framed as soft (and of course 'ineffective'), it has also occasionally been labelled as criminogenic – rehabilitation efforts according to this logic cause crime (Bidinotto 1994). Whilst this is not the dominant view, it is popular and thrives in an arena which has been unable to, in the public's eyes, refute the 'nothing works' doctrine.

This 'refuting' is vital for theatre practitioners who believe the arts have a role in this arena. Clearly, individuals involved in the 'what works' debate who dispute Martinson's findings need to dismiss simplistic divisions of soft and hard, and avoid debates that use it as their framework. An over-reliance on this dichotomy in the politics of criminal justice, is partly a reaction to a disputed claim and therefore, should not become an accepted boundary of discourse. Although the evidence-based practice championed in recent years has its own problems,[2] it provides a far more comfortable space within which theatre practice may be debated, grow and develop.

2   My concern, amongst others, is that the requirements for effectiveness may be used to stultify innovation and experimentation in programme design. If only certain programmes are given the stamp of approval, other approaches could be squeezed out.

DISPUTING MARTINSON – THE MAJOR FEATURES OF COGNITIVE BEHAVIOURAL GROUPWORK

Almost as soon as Martinson made his famous claim, several researchers started disputing his findings (see Andrews and Bonta 1994) and a number of years later he too recanted (Martinson 1979). Subsequently in extensive studies, such as the one by Lipsey (1992), programme evaluation data (in a meta-analysis where disparate studies are combined to create comparable information) was explored to ascertain whether it did in fact demonstrate any positive or negative effects. These studies showed that many programmes were positive whilst others had a zero or negative impact. In addition to countering the 'nothing works' argument, these meta-analyses aimed to distinguish what common features were held by 'successful' programmes. These features were to be a possible blueprint for future programme development. A number of researchers have now used these to make up 'effective intervention criteria' lists (see Gendreau 1996; McGuire and Priestley 1985), or design whole offender rehabilitation packages (see Ross and Fabiano 1985) and it is these that are fuelling much of the current practice.

Whilst the use of meta-analyses has concentrated on those programmes and interventions which have demonstrated positive effects on those that pass through them, it is important to also note briefly the interventions that faired less well. This is for two primary reasons. First, new interventions, and certainly theatre-based interventions, should be designed to avoid what is said not to 'work', as well as be based on what is said to 'work'. Second, in entering the debates surrounding criminal justice we need to counter any challenge to the effectiveness of our proposals with a demand to know the effectiveness of what is being suggested in their place. Unsurprisingly, punitive interventions do not show good results. The most punitive approaches – such as 'shock incarceration' where young people are given an aggressive dose of the horrors of prison – have negative effects. They increase the likelihood that a person will be re-arrested or re-offend (see Palmer 1996, p.135). They ultimately create more victims and make society more dangerous. Even if there were no evidence to support a less punitive intervention, a challenge can be made to the empirical basis of the enthusiasm for any alternatives.

POSITIVE INTERVENTIONS – EFFECTIVE PROGRAMMES

Whilst, as I have outlined above, the less successful interventions are important to understand, the interventions which have demonstrated positive impact on participants are those that have done the most to counter the 'nothing works' philosophy of Martinson. Although there are different emphases in the data, many commentators and subsequently practitioners have concluded that a cognitive behavioural approach to offender rehabilitation, or programmes that include a cognitive behavioural element are the most promising (Gendreau 1996; Andrews and Bonta 1994). These programmes, although not uniform, will generally include exercises which seek to challenge the thinking used by offenders to support their actions. This may be, for example, by examining group member's value systems or more specifically, the way they justify their crimes or minimise the impact of their behaviour on victims. Programmes of this nature concentrate on victim empathy, perspective taking, thinking errors, and decision making (see McGuire and Priestley 1985, for a comprehensive break-down). Overall, the locus of control is placed firmly with the offender, who may start to think differently, understanding his/her thoughts, and develop the complementary social skills in order to avoid re-offending. Cognitive behavioural programmes also include many offence-specific initiatives such as sex offender treatment, chemical dependency or anger management groups. The settings can be community, residential or secure and the work has been done with all ages.

Along with cognitive behavioural interventions, Palmer (1996) outlines several other promising interventions that are relevant here. Education was shown to have had a positive effect in two out of the three programme studies and employment programmes were viewed as one of the single most effective interventions. Another positive programme type, although difficult to define, is 'life skills'. These programmes use a variety of training methods to improve education, social and coping skills, and are linked to both the purely educational and the cognitive behavioural programming. An interesting aside about some of these programmes and also an area called 'social case work', is that they were often deemed more positive when they were not connected to the criminal justice system. Palmer states that 'Lipsey (1992) found that casework services that occurred outside the justice system had substantial impact on delinquency', whilst those within the system had a predominantly negative effect. Similarly, employment programmes seemed to have little effect on recidivism when a part of justice programmes, and again 'life skill' intervention 'within the nonjustice area…was the most successful one by far' (Palmer 1996, p.143).

Besides type of programme, the meta-analyses have also shown certain common implementation features that appear necessary for optimum impact. These are important because they pertain to the organisation, delivery and management of programmes. A cognitive behavioural course may exist but if it is not implemented in a certain way it is not likely to succeed. The first feature worth mentioning is that programmes must be responsive and delivered in a style that matches the cognitive skill of the client. A shy or disturbed individual is going to need a different input from an extremely verbal and extroverted person. This does not necessarily mean the work should not challenge the cognitive skills of the client, but that it should evolve and develop from them. A vital part of this responsivity is of course the concurrent matching of the facilitator, staff member or therapist to the client's and the programme's style. While staff must be 'interpersonally sensitive' (Gendreau 1996, p.123), so must the whole presentation and delivery of a programme. These points are clearly relevant for the delivery of the programmes in this edition and the design of these programmes was based on the need to offer different learning styles to clients.

A second point to mention here is the importance given to the way the activities are organised. The staff team needs to have bought into the philosophy behind a programme and be adequately trained to deliver it. For Blagg! and Pump! it is not only knowing the mechanics of the exercises, but also knowing why the exercises are being used. Programmes need to be delivered by individuals who are committed to them. The meta-analysis research indicates the need for programme integrity. Deviation from what a session intended to cover can mean that overall aims and objectives are less likely to be met. Whilst it is wrong to see this (or implement this) as a clamp on creative and flexible practice, it does mean that a programme is more likely to reach its target if, to put it simply, it delivers what it says it will. The detailed manuals presented in this edition, are part of this process of developing positive implementation procedures. Such procedures should be based on sound staff training and integrity in programme delivery.

The above represents a very rapid sketch of the 'what works' field, ending with notes on effective practice. This is the field in which theatre practitioners have taken a number of steps. They have been aided by the clear cross-over in practice and terminology and it is to this that I will now turn.

THEATRE AND OFFENDER REHABILITATION

Anyone with a theatre background who reads the seminal UK offender treatment book *Offending Behaviour* (McGuire and Priestley 1985) will note that it resembles many familiar theatre games books in its content and layout (see Spolin 1963; Boal 1992). At first glance, this comparison is purely formal and perhaps superficial, but the more mindful one is of the link when reading materials in this field, the more significant the bridge between the two disciplines becomes. The Anger Management Programme of the Alternative Learning Center, a school for suspended youth in Austin, Texas, is divided into exercises, role plays, and warm-ups which almost exactly mirror the format of creative drama workshops (Williams 1996). The significant bridge here becomes a major methodological overlap. Part of the explicit intention of this book is to give it more attention – to look at the bridge, the link, the overlap, and how each can inform the understanding and practice of the other.

Cognitive behavioural analysis of human action is one in which events, thoughts and then subsequent actions are shown to be interrelated and mutually reliant. To put it simply, a situation leads to a thought, which is processed into a decision, which is then put into action. The exact nature of the thought will depend on the familiarity of the incident, how it has been responded to in the past and reflection on the results of those previous actions. This process can become cyclical with repeated or similar incidents producing a standard response. A person is said to benefit from cognitive behavioural therapy when there is a 'fault' in that chain of events. This might be an over rigid tendency to view subjective interpretation and opinion as objective fact. It might be that the cycle is one of problematic or increasingly distressing behaviour. In a sense there is a 'fault' in learning or socialisation. For a person such as this, a situation may lead to misguided cognition, which in turn leads to a misguided decision and results in an inappropriate action. In the world of offending behaviour, this could mean an advance by a stranger is (mis)interpreted as a threat, the decision is made to avoid attack and personal injury, and the resulting action is that the stranger is assaulted. These misguided cognitions are referred to as 'thinking errors' or 'cognitive distortions', and if targeted for change, may help a person to avoid 'inappropriate action' (such as offending).

This brief summary hints at a connection between a theatrical process and cognitive behavioural theory. The chain can easily be applied to what happens when an actor is both performing and in training. A scripted scene relies on prompting motivations in a character to act in a certain way. An improvised scene requires in the actor the ability to respond to a situation and act spontaneously in an appropriate way (or inappropriate, depending on the situation/play). Acting training increases the ability of the actor to create artificial chains of cognition for situations and characters with whom they are not necessarily familiar. The actor is constantly asked to replace their cognitive process with someone else's and engage in decision making and action which is not their own. Their acting is clearly linked to their own life, but they are also trained or able to improvise (see Keith Johnstone 1985) and be spontaneous (see Moreno 1983) in the way they approach situations, real or otherwise. The creation of the act therefore, whether criminal or theatrical, is a related process. Kenneth Burke's 'five key terms of dramatism' could easily be applied to an analysis of a crime incident. They are: 'What was done (Act), when or where it was done (Scene), who did it (Agency), and why (Purpose)' (quoted in Carlson, 1996, p.36).

Although this connection can be partly explained by the fact that cognitive behavioural theory explains human interaction, and drama or theatre is, a performance or demonstration of human interaction; the link should not be minimised. There is a strong contention that everyday life is 'staged' (see Carlson 1996, p.36), and that 'everyday life' (Goffman 1959) is performed. 'Criminal action' exists within these performed boundaries but its performative nature is heightened by the frequent presence of planning and rehearsal, audience (whether they be immediate family, 'witnesses' or the public through the media), and social response. Erving Goffman takes up these themes when he defines performance as: 'all the activity of an individual which occurs during a period marked by his continuous presence before a particular set of observers and which has some influence on the observers' (Goffman, 1959, p.22).

There are many areas related to criminal justice that would fall into this definition. Criminal acts themselves clearly impact on those that observe them. Sentencing done to deter others is a performance event seeking to influence the observing public. Deterrence is clearly aimed beyond the individual offender. Giving a person a long sentence is often explicitly done in order to impact on a social audience. Similarly, the prisoner is continually observed by the guards, but also symbolically by a wider society that likes to 'see justice being done'. In Goffman's definition, therefore, criminal action and social reaction clearly enter the domain of performance.

Equally importantly, and perhaps more directly connected to theories of behaviour, the definition of performance offered by theatre researcher Richard Schechner, offers a key to understanding the meeting of theatre and offending behaviour. For Schechner, performance is 'twice-behaved behaviour' or 'restored' behaviour (quoted in Reinelt and Roach 1992, p.12). Behaviour becomes performance when it is either repeated, reinstated or rehearsed. The wedding, the football match and many other social manifestations become moments of performance within this analysis. The definition is clearly related to a cognitive behavioural analysis of human behaviour as cyclical, learnt and repeated (see Sheldon 1995, pp.44*ff*). People who rob a bank do not invent this activity for the first time. They learn it from a variety of sources and perform it when they enter the bank. The concept of learnt behaviour is therefore a crucial cross-over between two disciplines and deserves more detailed examination.

THE CHARACTERS LEARN A ROLE

It is widely argued (Hollin 1990; Sheldon 1995) that behaviour is learnt, and although chromosomes and biology may play a role, the interaction between humans and the immediate environment, is frequently viewed as the key to how a person conducts his/her life. A person's thoughts and decisions therefore do not spontaneously erupt from some hidden pathology, but are developed over years in response to previous environmental and life experiences. If an action is rewarded, or fulfils needs, or simply has no adverse effect, the cognitive and decision-making process is endorsed as appropriate. If this learning is strengthened through frequent repetition, a situation may provoke a very rapid response, as the thinking has become well-rehearsed. For many people, certain social situations become 'hard wired' to a certain reaction.

The concept of learnt behaviour is closely connected to theatre, because as mentioned above, it crosses over with definitions of performance and also implies a learning of roles. The variety of social roles that humans play over many years are practised and rehearsed until they 'become' behaviour. The exhibition of that learnt behaviour is linked to the enactment of 'restored' behaviour as described by Schechner. There is no simple distinction, however, between role rehearsal and eventual enactment. In fact, it is difficult to define the boundaries between the two. Nietzsche comments that 'if a person wants to seem to be something stubbornly and for a long time, he eventually finds it hard to be anything else' (Carlson 1996, p.42). A prisoner who ran the internal television station in San Quentin prison, California, recommended I listen to the rap song by E40 and the Click called 'Practice Looking Hard'. This song explained how young men rehearse their look before acting it out on the street.[3] The eventual 'finding it hard to be anything else' is the difficult learning process whereby a practised role becomes indistinguishable from subsequent behaviour. That process is also the key to behavioural change.

Acting training has always been about taking on and shedding roles. Sometimes they are close to your own personality and sometimes they differ greatly. One of the major objectives of offending behaviour groupwork is to make offenders 'act' differently, by challenging their cognitive processes, their values, and their attitudes. Traditionally, this is done by identifying problematic situations, discussing different modes of and cycles of behaviour in those familiar situations, confronting the distorted view of certain incidents or relationships, and planning for the future. The rehearsal process for both a

3   Interview conducted in San Quentin March 1997.

scripted and improvised play can be very similar to this process. Developing your knowledge of a character within the context of the creation or rehearsal of a complex narrative, concentrates on many similar processes. Role taking and narrative rehearsal provides a perfect opportunity to be another person, demonstrate alternative attributes, or explore unfamiliar actions. If offenders have a fixed set of characteristics and fixed, learnt responses, then a process that develops their skills in playing alternative roles, improvising new responses, and understanding and reacting more appropriately to others' actions, is targeting exactly the requirements of a rehabilitative intervention. Theatre practice, in a general sense of role development, plot/narrative creation, and conflict exploration and rehearsal; can therefore undermine fixed 'criminal characteristics' and 'criminal action' by offering new characters and new kinds of behaviour. Whilst it is important to note that role development is only a rehearsal (see the section on rehearsal later), the process itself is revelatory, transformative and if it is practised, it could become 'hard to become anything else'.

While the above discussions offer a general outline of connections between the two fields, I now want to make some more specific observations and also suggest ways in which theatrical methodologies are already used in offender rehabilitation programmes. This will lead to a discussion about how this 'use' often misses some of the key aspects of a theatre process, and how particular approaches to theatre teaching and practice can enrich the work of offender treatment programmes.

STEREOTYPED BEHAVIOUR

> Some individuals end up breaking the law because they react to particular social encounters in an inappropriate or stereotyped way. (McGuire and Priestley 1985, p.20)

> (T)he phrase 'criminal conduct' more strongly implies the violation of deeply held and widely shared norms than does the phrase 'criminal behaviour'. (Andrews and Bonta 1994, p.1)

Describing behaviour as stereotyped implies that it is not authentic – it is false or more importantly, not performed very well. A stereotype is a characterisation that heightens certain aspects of a personality, or simplifies certain behavioural responses. It tends to refer to a person's negative rather than to his/her positive attributes. Here it is also being used to imply that offenders stereotype themselves by performing their own behaviour to relatively simple routines, or restrict themselves to a predictable or limited set of responses. The key point for the purpose of this work is that offenders and offending are linked into discussions of performance and role.

In the quotation from Andrews and Bonta, the decision to discuss criminal conduct rather than criminal behaviour is, I believe, an inference that offenders' behaviour is perhaps more artificial, rehearsed or performed than other learnt behaviours. The choice of the word 'conduct' implies a thought and motivation, and perhaps a context (or an audience) to which it is played. Conduct seems more willed, intended, whereas behaviour is viewed as somehow more instinctive. It is perhaps more accurately the repeated or 'restored' behaviour discussed earlier. Whilst Andrews and Bonta use this phrase to distance themselves from notions of environmental crime causation, to me it also implies something about the nature of the criminal act. It is a conduct, a routine, and a performance.

The assertion that young or adult offenders are stereotyped in the way they deal with social situations, the way they problem solve or the way they present themselves to their peers; implies a limited ability to think creatively or to take on roles with depth or credibility. The way someone responds to daily challenges becomes predictable and may be inappropriate. They conduct themselves in a particular 'pre-prepared' way. For example, the violent offender who says that if someone looks at him in a certain way, he has to hit him or her. Or a male abuser's idea that if his wife does not do as he tells her the first time, he gives her a slap and 'that will make her do it'. These are not spontaneous one-off events, but repeated incidents. They often represent the stock response to the situation. They are a learnt and then practised routine. As I mentioned above, they are the hard-wired response.

The assertion made above that this behaviour is learnt, implies that it can be un- or relearnt. If it is an action – a three-dimensional, moving, interacting form of behaviour (not information, facts, or figures) that is learnt, practised, performed – then the unlearning or relearning must be focused more on the apprehension of new actions and rehearsing of new routines. The response of violence, for example, is a complex, learnt behaviour or performance. You may have seen it in your childhood over and over again, you might have experienced it yourself repeatedly, you might have tried it out as a child and then you might have practised it thoroughly as an adult. This process engages all your self – your sight, hearing, emotions, physique, and thinking. To develop non-violent responses it would appear logical that a similar process needs to be used. If the way a behaviour has been learnt is complex, the way it is unlearnt and the way that new conducts are found must have similar complexity and multi-sensory impact. I am of course hinting at how an offender treatment programme should be structured. Being given a lecture on violence will only engage one part of the mind, and barely scrape the surface of the many other ways that behaviour is understood and enacted. To me the logical process is an intensely theatrical process. Offender treatment programmes need a systematised use of theatre techniques to train in complex role taking, different kinds of behaviour and innovative non-stereotyped routines.

ROLE PLAY AND MODELLING

The idea that offenders have a learning history that leads to simplified responses to frequently occurring situations, implies that they have little spontaneity or ability to improvise freely. It is perhaps wrong to characterise this as a problem of 'offenders' only, since responding in set ways is a component of many individuals' personalities. It is not that offenders exhibit one personality trait whilst law-abiding others perform differently. There is a continuum of problem-solving abilities that can in many ways be linked to levels of moral reasoning (see Kohlberg 1976). Although these levels have a tendency to be over-prescriptive and culturally and historically specific, they emphasise that reasoning, thinking and thus problem solving are best understood as a changing process rather than an either/or.

Whilst all forms of fixed or stereotyped behaviour can be damaging or limiting, such responses in offenders can lead to a great deal of pain and hurt. 'Offending behaviour' tends to be that which impacts negatively on individuals, families and communities. The context in which role learning has taken place might have included a situation in which violence was a common approach to problem solving, where men's aggressiveness or perhaps impulsiveness were reinforced, where 'role models' were delinquent peers rather than 'appropriate adults'. The performance options have thus developed in a particular direction, and may have been restricted in their diversity. This is not necessarily unique to a special category called 'offender', but common in many aspects of social life. We all play different roles at different times of our life and sometimes at different times of the day. We are father/mother, son/daughter, neighbour, and worker in a matter of hours. As touched on above, a rich and diverse mix of social and environmental history, personal temperament and potential, and the gradual practice of each role *in situ* over time, determine the script of each of these roles. My performance as father is inspired by sources such as my own father, other friends who are fathers, the way my partner parents and so on. There are multiple influences and they inform each other. One of the keys to role play in everyday life is the variety of sources or role models a person may have, the flexibility each of these has in itself and the degree to which roles can learn to adapt and change. It is false to assume that all these roles in our life are separate and isolated. Ideally they should freely flow between each other. Role play in the theatre rehearsal sense develops participants' ability to draw on experience in a flexible and creative way. It is this quality that role play in the therapeutic context should be exploring. It champions spontaneity[4] against rigidity.

In the offending behaviour literature, limited role-taking abilities are noted (Hollin 1990, pp.69–70, Chandler 1973; pp.326–332) as relevant to the offender population and therefore an important aspect of treatment. Role play is in fact a major part of a number of rehabilitation programmes (McGuire and Priestley 1985, pp.28–30; Rose 1998, p.239; Goldstein and Glick 1994, p.55) and there is widespread acceptance that role play can add to their effectiveness. Palmer notes a report by Gottschalk *et al.* (1987) which described a 'successful outcome for 45 per cent of 20 studies where modelling/role playing was included' (Palmer 1996, p.142). However, it is important to note that the positive use of role play can be undermined by criminal justice processing where there is an inherent limiting of individual role-taking abilities and a negative reinforcement and solidification of certain behaviours. It is important to emphasise Lipsey's finding that 'more as opposed to less, criminal justice processing was associated with slightly increased recidivism rates. This finding was mildly consistent with labelling theory, and inconsistent with deterrence theory' (Lipsey 1989, quoted in Andrews and Bonta 1994, p.189). I would argue that punitive responses to crime and particularly prison sentences tend to emphasise one role in the person to the detriment of all others. A prison sentence and the prison regime encourage a person to play the role of prisoner, offender and criminal twenty-four hours a day, as opposed to father, son, daughter, friend, colleague and so on. Joe White, an ex-prisoner who was actively involved in theatre for his whole time in prison, elaborates on this when he explains in detail how prison life strips you of your full and rounded identity (White 1998). It leaves you performing a one-dimensional version or aspect of yourself. The acceptance of role play in offending behaviour programmes is thus promising but they are often situated in an environment that has the opposite effect.

Besides the problem of the situational impact on programme objectives, whilst many offending behaviour programmes do recognise the value of role play, they do not fully develop the potential of an open role rehearsal process. They maintain a control that prevents spontaneity and a real challenge to fixed roles. This can be seen more clearly in a detailed look at the approach offered

---

4   See Moreno (1983) for full discussion of spontaneity.

by Arnold Goldstein, the Director for the Center for Research on Aggression at Syracuse University, US. He has developed a programme called 'Aggression Replacement Training' (ART) which has been used with adolescents, youths at risk and US gangs (Goldstein and Glick 1994). I do not dispute the claim that '(ART) appears to promote skill acquisition and performance, improves anger control, decreases the frequency of acting-out behaviors, and increases the frequency of constructive, prosocial behaviors' (Goldstein and Glick 1994, p.72). The programme is clearly well structured, implemented widely and has demonstrated positive outcomes. It should be applauded in particular because it includes many active participatory exercises and does not involve only the lecturing or didactic approach that I criticised above. It is immediately obvious, for example, from the quote above that Goldstein is interested in the 'performance' of learnt skills and changing the ways people 'act-out'. He implies a performative quality to his work without expressly recognising it. I am wary, however, of this programme's use of role play and theatrical techniques, and this illustrates my general disquiet about some of the elements of behaviour modification programmes.

Goldstein uses an approach to social skills training he calls 'skillstreaming' (Goldstein and Glick 1994, p.53). It is a very precise version of a technique called behaviour rehearsal used by behaviour therapists (see for example Goldfried and Davison 1979 for a detailed description of behaviour rehearsal). A session is broken down in to four sections:

1   Modelling

2   Role playing

3   Performance feedback

4   Transfer of training (Goldstein and Glick 1994 p.53).

These are very similar to Goldfried and Davison's four stages of behaviour rehearsal:

1   Preparation

2   Selection of target situation

3   Behaviour rehearsal proper

4   Using new roles in real life (Goldfried and Davison 1979, p.136).

A first concern is with the modelling sequence itself (see also Rose 1998). Goldstein and Glick write that 'trainees first be exposed to expert examples of the behaviours we want them to learn' (Goldstein and Glick 1994, p.54). The behaviour under examination is broken down 'into four to six behavioural steps'. The trainees are the passive recipients of information. Whilst as demonstrated on 'The Skillstreaming Video' the students can input into the subject matter, the behavioural boundaries to be taught are decided beyond the group. This increases the likelihood that the training does not cover exactly what the trainees need, nor does it include them in the valuable exploration of what are problem behaviours in their eyes. If the debate were to be opened with an exploration of self-defined problems – what do they struggle with in their real lives? – they would be positively involved in what is a problem- solving exercise rather than be left as recipients of more 'expert' knowledge to be accepted or rejected. If the expertise is located outside their experience from the first instance, it will continue to be difficult to incorporate it into their personal behaviour. It is an external addition rather than an organic part, arriving out of their own process of discovery. They are being taught the concrete thinking skill of accepting rather than the more imaginative skill of developing thinking for themselves.

Treating behaviour as a human interaction that can be broken down into isolated moments to be learnt, denies the complexity of it as a lived experience. The behaviour cannot simply be parcelled in a way that is devoid of context, the characters involved and the history of the narrative. Behaviour rehearsal in the 'laboratory conditions' of groupwork has to be profoundly aware of the narrative context from which it has been extracted. The participants need to be constantly bringing the complexities and contradictions of their real worlds to bear on the situation under the microscope.

In a sense, the criticism here is about who controls the script of the therapeutic process. If we are trying to challenge the thinking of our group and develop rich social skills, they have to be developers of the rehearsal script rather than just actors who learn the roles by rote. McGuire and Priestley make this very clear when they state that the methods used in offending behaviour groupwork 'must be placed under the control of those who are trying to change themselves' (McGuire and Priestley 1985, p.21). This is the second area of concern to discuss and it is linked very clearly to the first. Goldstein, in setting up the role plays, does not establish them as problem solving in themselves. The answer – the correct way of behaving in a given situation – is given at the beginning and the group have to copy or learn it. Pedagogically this is weak. Role play can also be used to dig for solutions and alternatives. McGuire and Priestley hint at this as their support for a developmental role for the groupwork leader, when 'people…have difficulty imitating models effectively' (1985, p.100). In these situations they should act as coaches, gently encouraging the participants while they are role playing. Whilst preferable, this still implies a fixed skill to be honed. The process is still one of imitation rather than discovery. If the group were allowed to illustrate the problem behaviour at the beginning, the process could then be to use role play to act out and thus reveal possible alternatives. These alternatives can then be rejected or accepted by the group as a whole, including the therapist/trainer. The process encourages the group to solve the problem and therefore, in its very style is encouraging the creative thinking with which offending behaviour programmes should be concerned. The feedback process, in this way, does not become a test of 'the adequacy of [the participants'] performance' (Goldfried and Davison 1979, p.144), but a test by the whole group as to whether the new behaviour would be possible in a real world setting.

The concept of the 'standard for social adequacy' used by Goldfried and Davison to describe the target set for the behaviour or performance of their clients (1979, p.147), hints at my more general anxiety about this use of role play. If we design programmes that have preordained standards of behaviour, we very easily encourage one of the attributes which we are trying to avoid. Teaching a fixed standard behaviour encourages further fixed or rigid thinking and behaving. It attempts to replace one set of concrete behaviours with another and therefore does not challenge the core problem that is the stereotypical response to social problems. Magnified to a macro level, we enter the realms of the ethics of behaviour modification.[5] Andrews and Bonta note that 'correctional programs should not attempt to produce "perfect people" according to some standard of perfection' (1994, p.203). Modelling by setting standards in the ways described by many of the offending behaviour theorists (Goldstein and Glick, Rose, McGuire and Priestley), is in danger of doing just that. Andrews and Bonta contradict their own assertion when they state that 'it is interesting that Shure and Spivak (82) also contend that teaching individuals "how" to think and not "what" to think will lead to people making the right decision…we are less inclined to this view' (1994, p. 143). They counter their own edict with their belief that teaching to a standard is appropriate. As I have outlined above, teaching people what to think will lead to a continuation of stereotyped behaviour and will also start to move into the realms of creating 'perfect people'. A 'Brave New World' I would hope groupworkers do not want to move towards.

---

5   I use that expression 'behaviour modification' deliberately because it jars. It conjures up in my mind unethical and highly dubious processes associated with oppressive regimes and unscrupulous psychologists!

STANDING IN ANOTHER'S SHOES: ROLE REVERSAL AND PERSPECTIVE TAKING

Two other important concepts within cognitive behavioural courses that are closely linked to theatrical processes are role reversal and perspective taking. McGuire and Priestley state that 'the ability to "take the role of another" is one of the foundations of moral maturity. An inability to do so may be at the root of some offending behaviour' (McGuire and Priestley 1985, p.48). One of the basic premises of acting, that of taking the role of another, is highlighted as central in offending behaviour work. If a person can stand in the shoes of someone else it is argued that they are more likely to temper their own, perhaps extreme views, or at least see the world from the perspective of another. This would counter the perceived tendency for offenders to have a very egocentric orientation[6] (Andrews and Bonta 1994, p.87) and offer them an understanding of the impact of their behaviour on others. If a vital part of a rehabilitative process is developing insight into the effect of your actions on others, particularly your victims, then role reversal would appear to play a key role.

The emphasis on 'role reversal' is a familiar part of the psychodrama process where role swapping is a key practice. A person who is recreating a situation with another may swap with that person, so as to gain insight into their perspective. In the case of psychodrama this would usually be a significant person in their lives – a father, lover, or mother – with whom they had an unresolved conflict. Whilst this direct exchange is important, role reversal is too narrow a definition of what should be a central process in rehabilitative groupwork. Returning to the concern with the stereotypical behaviours of offenders, it is not the replacement with another role that would offer an alternative, but an ability to be fluent in multiple roles. So the role of the other is not important in itself. It is not enough to simply ask a person to play the role of their victim and 'see how it feels' (see Thompson 1998b). It is the skill to take on numerous roles in appropriate situations, and understand social encounters from a variety of perspectives. It is the difference between teaching someone to read a sentence and developing literacy.

The clinical psychologist, Chandler, conducted one of the most interesting experiments exploring this theme in 1973. It is worth examining this in some detail. He designed 'an experimental program which employed drama and the making of video film as a vehicle for providing remedial training in role taking' (Chandler 1973, p.326). The initial assessment of the participants in the experiment used perspective-taking cartoon exercises to understand

---

6   I use the word 'perceived' because I am uncomfortable with the reductionist use of generalisations about 'offenders' temperaments'.

differences in their role-taking skills. This involved each individual being shown a cartoon sequence in which a character clearly could not have known an aspect of the story. Those with lower perspective-taking ability were less able to indicate when a newly arrived character would and would not know previous plot detail. Significantly, those young people who were designated delinquent 'typically demonstrated marked deficits in their ability to differentiate their own point of view from that of others' (Chandler 1973, p.329). The experiment involved two groups of young people, forty-five designated delinquents and forty-five designated as non-delinquents.[7] Whilst fifteen from each group were put in a control group, the other thirty from each group were given a summer programme consisting of three-hour daily sessions during a ten-week block. The thirty young people were then split between two activities. Fifteen from each group were 'encouraged to develop, portray and record brief skits dealing with events involving persons their own age' (Chandler 1973, p.328). They had to be about real life situations rather than episodes involving television or film characters. In addition, every participant had to have a part, scenes had to be re-run so everyone occupied every role in the plot, and the video recording had to be viewed in order to make improvements. This was the 'experimental group'.[8] The other fifteen from each delinquent and non-delinquent group were a placebo. They were instructed to make videos and cartoons on their own neighbourhood with the restriction that they did not repeatedly review their material and that participants were not to be 'subjects of their own film making efforts' (Chandler 1973, p.329).

In post-test follow-up, the subjects from the experimental group committed roughly half the 'delinquencies' of both the placebo and the control groups. This could not be accounted for by a 'good time' factor of enjoying the activity and meeting new people because, according to Chandler, both the placebo and the experimental group were committed to their activities. The implication is that their role-taking ability increased and with it came a wider perspective that prevented them from engaging in delinquent behaviour. Chandler concludes his report by stating that: 'the results of this study do suggest the utility of attempting to understand delinquent youth in terms of their developmental progress in the acquisition of certain formal, sociocognitive operations

7   I use the word 'designated' specifically to imply I do not know how they were given this label and such designation is clearly problematic.

8   There are ethical dilemmas about experiments that impact directly on young people's lives, and therefore my use of Chandler's study as an example does not infer an agreement with his methodology.

necessary for the effective solution of important human interaction problems' (Chandler 1973, p.332).

Put simply, their role-taking abilities are poor and thus in developing their role play skills, they would be more able to deal effectively with difficult situations in the future.

There are a number of key points to be drawn from this study. First, in the difference between the placebo and the experimental group. It would appear that a group who were asked to play and rehearse roles which were part of their lives developed wider perspective-taking abilities than those that were asked to simply video their neighbourhood and make cartoons. Playing *relevant* roles is therefore key to developing these skills. This offers a possible guideline to arts practice engaged with communities, because arts work *per se* did not have the desired impact here. The active representation and exploration of their own lives was vital. In saying relevant roles however, I am deliberately hinting at the next point to be made. What roles would have been relevant? Did the roles have to be ones with which they were familiar or was it the situations and dilemmas that these roles inspired that were significant? From the study it would be difficult to make firm conclusions, but these questions are important for theatre practitioners because the answers could offer clues to best practice. Do the groups have to enact naturalistic dramas of their own lives or could the rehearsing of *Romeo and Juliet* develop similar role-taking and thus perspective-taking abilities. The relationship between Romeo and Juliet, and the decisions they struggled with might be very relevant to many groups of young people. The work outlined in the following pages is closer to the former approach, but this does not by default dismiss the latter.

The third point to make about the importance of Chandler's study concerns the notion of rehearsal. New behaviour is not learnt by someone describing or telling you about it, nor does it become incorporated into your own life by simple enactment. Rehearsal is a vital part of the process if there is not to be what Goldstein and Glick call 'the failure of generalisation of gain' (Goldstein and Glick 1994, p.100). Goldstein and Glick believe this failure evolves from an assumption that the therapeutic process in itself should 'inoculate' participants against future problems. This clearly does not happen in a large number of the researched programmes in this field and 'much more often than not, transfer and maintenance of intervention gains [does] not occur' (Goldstein and Glick, 1994 p.102). Rather than the medical model of one-off inoculation to offer protection for the future, it is the theatrical model of repetition and rehearsal that is important. Again a key theatrical concept becomes central to the offender treatment process.

Rehearsal is thus vital to ensure that lessons from the groupwork room are transferred to the world outside. In the wider offender rehabilitation literature this is often referred to as 'relapse prevention' (see Gendreau 1996, p.125) and interestingly, Goldstein and Glick rename it 'overlearning' (1994, p104). It is 'overdoing it' rather than doing it thoroughly. Rehearsal is thus explained, rather elaborately, in the following terms: 'Overlearning, also known as *maximising response availability*, involves requiring the trainee to engage in repeated *successful* practice of the newly learned (skill) behaviors, in contrast to moving onto new lessons once initial success on the first behavior is shown' (italics in original) (Goldstein and Glick 1994, p.103).

This was 'operationalized by requiring participants to role play and re-role play' (Goldstein and Glick 1994, p.104). A procedure familiar to many students of theatre. Similarly, Gendreau explains a 'relapse prevention' initiative where elements of the strategy include the following:

1   Plan and rehearse alternative prosocial responses.

2   Monitor and anticipate problem situations.

3   Practice new prosocial behaviors in increasingly difficult situations and reward improved competencies… (Gendreau 1996, p.125).

Although in both Goldstein and Glick and Gendreau, the process appears prescriptive, it does back up Chandler's insistence that repetition can increase role-taking abilities generally.

So in order to stand in another's shoes and to take the perspective of other people or more specifically, a victim of your behaviour, a theatrical process is vital. There is valuable evidence that an extended use of role play and role reversal can be an important part of this process. It is not only that theatricalising aspects of your life and repeating or rehearsing the scenarios, improves your understanding of others; but this understanding can also be incorporated into the way you interact with the world around you. Developing an awareness of other people's roles in a groupwork setting can affect the playing of your own role in the real world.

ECSTASY OR RATIONALITY?

I have mentioned role play and rehearsal as important components of offender treatment programmes and also hinted at the types of role play scenarios that might be most relevant. What has not been examined and what is certainly missed by most psychological approaches in this area, is the notion of acting itself. It is almost taken for granted that roles will simply be 'played' with no account of how they will be played and how different styles of playing make different connections to the actor's thoughts and emotions. There are a variety of acting traditions that need to be understood to incorporate role playing successfully into the rehabilitation process.

Two examples will help to illustrate this point. First, from a drama workshop in the Hindley Young Offender Institution in the North West of England.[9]

> Young men were encouraged to create a scene as the starting point for a story on issues of interest to them. They elected to recreate an armed robbery. Very soon the group (all aged between sixteen and twenty-one) were dressed in bandannas, holding mimed weapons and approaching the table which was now a bank counter. Much chaos ensued with bodies jumping across chairs, threatening shouts and physical but staged fights. The men were clearly totally involved and enjoying the experience.

The second example comes from a role play session witnessed at Marlin Orientation and Assessment Center, Texas.[10]

> The role play was of a drug dealing incident chosen by the caseworker. At all times the learning objectives of the activity were prioritised and it was emphasised that the participants should not try to win any 'academy awards'. They had to be 'mature' and only demonstrate their roles. All action was stylised and moments such as the passing of the drugs were done symbolically – through the slapping of hands. There was clearly a belief that they should not get over involved.

Phil Jones in his book *Drama as Therapy: Theatre as Living* (1996) outlines the tendency of Western thought to divide bodily expression between the Apollonian and the Dionysian, where the 'Apollonian expression emphasises the rational, discursive and analytic (and) Dionysian expression is characterised by rapture, sexual ecstasy and the frenzy of the body in dance' (Jones 1996, p.150). This division can be seen in the use of role play in the two examples above. One was strongly rational whilst the other resulted in an element of frenzy.

The degree to which actors or participants in role play sessions should maintain distance from their role or be consumed by them, is a central concern to theatre practitioners, dramatherapists, and should become central to the use of role play in offender rehabilitation and groupwork. This debate is often referred to in terms of 'rationality' and 'ecstasy' (Jones 1996, pp.199–202).

9   This took place in 1995 and these notes are taken from the video made of the workshop. A
      drama teacher employed by the education department of the institution ran the session.
10   25/11/96. This comes from my notes taken during the visit.

The ecstasy side of this equation is more often associated with the work of the Russian director and teacher of acting, Stanislavski (1863–1938). He based his work with actors on a close examination of the psychological development of character, an approach which Schechner calls 'performing by becoming or being possessed by another' (Schechner 1998, p.177, quoted in Jones 1996, p.200). Rationality in acting – maintaining a distance from your role – is more often associated with the German director and playwright, Bertol Brecht (1898–1956). A Brechtian-influenced acting style requires the actor to think and remain outside the role, critically reflecting on the action taken. This style, as demonstrated by the Texan example above, is more often associated with the therapeutic use of role play. Jones (1996, p.201) discusses Johnson and Johnson's work on group theory (1987) where the 'role taker stays fully aware of the reason for the activity, and is open to cognitive learning processes' (Jones 1996, p.201).

However, it is not as simple as opting for the objective, Brechtian-based approach to acting and role play, while dismissing the role immersion prompted by the Stanislavskian school. The Brazilian theatre director/ practitioner Augusto Boal, whose work I will discuss in greater depth later, explains that there is a need for a balance between 'rationality' and 'ecstasy'. He states that 'an intense emotion memory exercise…can be dangerous unless one afterwards "rationalises" what has happened' (Boal 1992, p.47). This would certainly be the case with the armed robbery enactment that is described above. Unless there were a post role play reflection on the experience, it is likely to have been counter-productive. This said, however, emotional involvement should not be dismissed as inappropriate in any circumstances. Balance is possible. There needs to be an awareness that both a distance from the subject and an emotional involvement in it, can be powerful parts of the therapeutic process.

One of the objectives of offender rehabilitation is to encourage participants to look critically at their own behaviour. With this in mind, it is important to encourage an acting style that develops a sense of distancing during role plays, when group members perform versions of themselves. The armed robbery allowed them to become immersed in their own real or desired behaviour and so provided a vicarious pleasure, enforcing the action rather than challenging it. A Brechtian approach here would emphasise the need for the actors to be in a constant state of distance from the characters they portray. In maintaining that distance, a process of reflection is possible.

Another objective of these programmes, however, is to develop victim empathy and an understanding of the impact of behaviour on others. Effective work has to be affective and for this it is important to develop a participant's close involvement with a character being role played. The process seeks to reveal the emotional and cognitive impact of an action on another person. Groupwork needs to encourage close involvement with a particular role when it involves somebody the group would not usually consider or for whom they have little sympathy. If the actor remains distant, they will never fully understand the emotional impact of their own behaviour on that person. If they are given the opportunity to immerse themselves in that character, new insights can be explored. For example, if the young men playing the armed robbers were encouraged to develop a 'Dionysian' portrayal of the bank clerk's life, the 'ecstasy' of the role play would have been less problematic. Immersion in the life of another person in a Stanislavskian sense, can be positive. Rather than a continued emotional attachment with the armed robbers (roles they were both comfortable with and desired), the role play could have pushed for a connection to be made with the experience and emotional trauma of the unfamiliar role. Although this process may not be inevitable or easy, it is an important to strive for this objective.

The key, therefore, in discussing these different approaches to 'acting' is to understand the power and effect of both styles. To develop empathy with a person, belief or behaviour, it is important for a participant to be(come) that person – physically and emotionally – as much as possible. To criticise a belief, a behaviour or an action, a person needs to develop some critical distance from it. They need to be able to witness it, reflect on it and remain detached from it. Groupwork that uses role play needs to account carefully for the purpose of each moment and to consider designing role play exercises appropriately. The style of role play used should be varied but dependent on the objectives of the session.

COGNITIVE DEXTERITY

Much cognitive behavioural groupwork is concerned with developing an individual's ability to think about situations clearly, so that they arrive at more pro-social decisions and actions. In teaching thinking or cognitive skills there is a problem, as I have outlined above, when the programme gives the 'destination' rather than develop an individual's ability to arrive or even set off on that journey. A rehearsal process that is pre-scripted by the therapist rather than scripted by the participant, becomes an exercise in learning the right way rather than discovering an appropriate one. If a person is making thinking errors – justifying their abuse of their partner, minimising the effects of their burgling – giving them alternative thoughts does not help their thinking in the long run. What Goldstein and Glick call 'maximising response availability' (Goldstein and Glick 1994, p.103) should be a learning objective of the process. Programmes should explicitly encourage a spontaneity in thinking rather than an unthinking acceptance of what is 'right'.

In Texas, the Youth Commission,[11] as part of their 'resocialization program', insists that all trainees learn a 'personal layout' which includes a statement about how their offence hurt their victim. They learn this by rote and perform it to visitors, staff and their peers. Whilst I have argued that rehearsal can be a positive part of offender rehabilitation, it is also vital to distinguish between different types of rehearsal. If the young people are actively engaged in the creation of the script, as seemed to be the case in the Chandler study, their ownership of the material means that they might develop their own role-taking and perspective-taking abilities through the process. However, it is difficult to argue that repeated performance automatically leads to an incorporation of the script into your own personality. Nietzsche's belief that you eventually become the role you repeat, hides the fact that 'eventually becoming' is a tough learning process. Unthinking repetition could lead to automaton-like concrete thinking. The young people in the Texas Youth Commission in the early months of their sentence, seemed to present their personal layouts with little hint of personal connection to the material.[12] An over-prescriptive and pre-scripted therapeutic process can lead to the development of very two-dimensional cognitive skills.

Programmes should be developing a cognitive dexterity – an ability for individuals to look at all possibilities; to respond to situations in a rich variety of ways; to be different in their thinking. Cognitive dexterity refers to a mental ability that is open, flexible and able to generate realistic solutions to complex problems. Insisting on a right way, limits this ability and inhibits the development of a mentally dextrous approach to social interactions. Cognitive dexterity means that an individual will look carefully at situations and be able to read different rather than singular meanings. It means that they should develop a rounded and agile role playing, which responds organically to a given situation rather than being grafted onto different social realities. Cognitive dexterity defies rigid thinking and prioritises flexibility and spontaneity. It insists on the weighing of all possible perspectives and encourages standing in others' shoes before actions are taken. It aims at decision-making and negotiation skills that fully understand the impact of our behaviour on others. Whilst physical dexterity implies an adroitness in one's

11   The juvenile justice department responsible for incarcerating ten to eighteen year olds.

12   From my observations during visits to Marlin Orientation and Assessment Center and Giddings State Home, Texas 1996/7.

bodily movements, cognitive dexterity implies a mental agility, constantly seeking for other ways and with an ability to celebrate doubt over certainty.

Cognitive dexterity is a process and a continuum. It is a state that should be encouraged without a clear and fixed idea of when it has been achieved. No one arrives at a final point of cognitive dexterity. It is not only relevant to the world of offender rehabilitation, but it is crucial in the whole field of education and groupwork. For offenders and prisoners, it allows them to imagine alternative roles for themselves. In a system that stigmatises and labels, and creates environments that encourage fixed and debilitating role taking, an attitude of cognitive dexterity provides the hope that people can be(come) someone else. Both the Blagg! and the Pump! programmes do not claim to be ideal versions of this process. However, they do seek to place the participant at the centre of the experience, and provide a possibility for the open development of thinking and role-taking skills.

THEATRICAL ASSUMPTIONS

The above description of cognitive dexterity and much of the discussion of theatre techniques and points made about groupwork, owe a great deal to the pedagogical theories of Paulo Freire and the theatre practice of Augusto Boal. It is important to make some of these connections explicit, because they are a central theme of the book. It would be inaccurate to assume that 'theatre' is a single construct when arguing for close links between offender rehabilitation approaches, more general groupwork and theatre. I have already mentioned briefly the debate about whether the rehearsal of a text such as *Romeo and Juliet* would have a similar impact on role-taking abilities as a naturalistic, group-developed scenario. Similarly, different schools of acting have been cited as affecting the impact of role play sessions. Whilst to argue the strength of one approach *against* the possibilities offered by another would be unproductive, there are important pedagogical and theatrical principles that are worth outlining – and which have already been implicit in much of this text.

LEARNING STYLE

Andrews and Bonta report that one of the criteria for effective interventions with offenders, is that treatment approaches are 'matched to the learning styles of the offenders' (Andrews and Bonta 1994, p.189). I have emphasised above that this should include a non-didactic style that includes participation and problem solving by the group. For people who have often struggled or failed in traditional education settings, the groupwork experience must involve them and value their input. Paulo Freire in his seminal work, *Pedagogy of the Oppressed* (Freire 1970), distinguishes between what he describes as a 'banking' educational system and a 'problem-posing' educational approach. Banking education treats students as objects to be filled with the knowledge of the expert teacher, whereas in 'problem-posing' education students are subjects of the process, developing 'their power to perceive critically the way they exist in the world with which and in which they find themselves' (Freire 1970, p.64). The pedagogical style of groupwork is therefore not simply an ethical decision about how to teach a group fairly, but it is central to how and what the group are going to learn. Problem-posing education 'affirms men and women as beings in the process of becoming' (Freire 1970, p.65) and this is exactly what state offender treatment should assume about the clients it works with. We cannot hope for personal change if the teaching style treats participants as objects to be filled with 'correct' ways of behaving. In encouraging people to 'become', we cannot have a pre-scripted idea of where they are going. The work of offender treatment professionals is to provide the resources for participants to develop open thinking, as implied by the term 'cognitive dexterity'.

PROBLEM-POSING THEATRE?

A problem-posing educational approach to offender treatment should use problem-posing theatrical techniques. A 'banking' theatre would require clients to watch role plays passively, have scripts written and new behaviour to be learnt decided for them in advance. They would be instructed to perform according to the strict requirements of the expert director. A problem-posing theatre would ensure that the division between those who observed and those who performed is broken. It would encourage a group to theatricalise their own stories and present the world, not as a fixed finished entity, but as a future to be created. This is the theatre of the Brazilian theatre practitioner, Augusto Boal, who wrote the book *Theatre of the Oppressed* (Boal 1979), deliberately aligning himself with the pedagogical tradition of his fellow Brazilian, Freire. To Boal, theatre is 'the art of looking at ourselves' (Boal 1992, p.xxx). To put it simply, 'looking at ourselves' is precisely the focus of much cognitive behavioural groupwork.

Whilst the work of Boal, from the general approaches outlined in *Games for Actors and Non-Actors* (1992) to the more therapeutic techniques of *Rainbow of Desire* (1995), informs the discussion within this introduction and most of the techniques explained in the following programmes; it is also important to discuss here how he offers a clue to the limits of cognitive behavioural work and perhaps how it should be extended. Boal makes it very clear that the drama workshop does not take the place of transformation, but is a rehearsal for a transformation – a 'rehearsal of revolution' (Boal 1979, p155). There is a direct and necessary link between the aesthetic space of the theatre, the therapeutic space of the treatment group and the outside world. Relapse prevention has already been discussed as a vital component of rehabilitation programmes. These techniques, however, are often seen to be problematic because there is great difficulty in controlling external social and environmental factors. The transferability of skills learnt and rehearsed in one place, is neither immediate nor simple. New behaviours and solutions discovered in the groupwork room do not necessarily translate into actions outside. The problem is of 'the failure of the generalisation of gain' (Goldstein and Glick 1994, p.102) mentioned above. 'Positive results' as explained in Howell 'often deteriorate after clients leave the programs' (Howell *et al.* 1995, p.166). The link between the rehearsal and the revolution is not necessarily direct, nor is it easy.

Boal insists that the particular concerns of individuals should be generalised so that they resonate with the majority of the group (Boal 1992). This is not something that should wait until after, but should be central to the process of the workshop. Whilst personal lessons may be drawn, it is the connections made to the wider group and social problems that are important. One person's story can thus become a model for the issues to be resolved for a whole group of people. This movement from the specific to the general is a key part of avoiding the weaknesses in relapse prevention or transference to the outside world. Clients need to be examining not just their own behaviour, but how their behaviour relates to other people and interacts with the wider society. Change on an individual level can only be maintained by examining how it relates to other's behaviour and social change more broadly. The therapeutic process must gradually shift focus from the individual to the individual in relation to their society. This needs to happen if the problem noted by Howell of positive results deteriorating after a person has left a programme, is not constantly repeated. Interventions cannot simply develop resilience to an environment that might stimulate problem behaviours, but they must also develop a resistance to that environment. That resistance is not just an inward-looking, tough, cognitively impervious shell, but an outward engagement with the society in which they are struggling. Individuals are better able to change themselves if they are committed to a project to change the community or society in which they reside. As I have stated elsewhere:

> the fear that many prisoners have of the power of their home environment
> to damage their best intentions to change, needs to be reframed by
> offering them the skills and confidence to change that environment. Whilst

this might seem a daunting task…even an engagement with the process of social change would provide a context for personal change to be sustained (Thompson 1998a, p.20)

Boal's theatre provides the practical insights and techniques to make this bridge. His latest work in 'legislative theatre' (Boal 1998) has pulled this full circle with an explanation of how theatre can be used by groups to directly impact the legislative programmes of governments. This is not separate work from the therapeutic but a vital part of a whole – a whole that recognises that individual change is vitally connected to community change, and that community change requires transformations in the citizens who make up that society.

CONCLUSIONS

The notes and noises made in this introduction – like the various educational and therapeutic processes they are describing – are profoundly unfinished. They are meant as a dialogue with a variety of disciplines that could and should be developed further. They are also meant as a dialogue with the practice described in the programmes that follow. Specifically, they sit in this edition as a counterweight to that practice. The programmes that are described here were devised long before this introduction was written and therefore they have a different history. The ideas outlined in the introduction have been developed, not only through the devising of these programmes, but also in response to their execution. The theory described here does not, therefore, in a simple deterministic fashion, reflect the practice of the programmes. The theoretical approach has developed from the process of running, watching and thinking about these programmes. It did not magically exist before, and therefore was not a measure against which the practice was evaluated from the outset.

I would like to see this dialogue continued – both in the practical exploration of the techniques described here and a further development through that practice of the ideas offered in this Introduction. Applied theatre can only progress if the negotiations between theatre and areas of social policy theory and practice are opened, extended and developed. Theatre practitioners have much to learn.

The Programme
and the Workshop

This book is concerned with two separate examples of applied theatre practice. The Blagg! offending behaviour workshop and the Pump! anger management programme. Both were created by the Theatre in Prisons and Probation (TIPP) Centre, but represent different moments in the organisation's history. Blagg! is, for example, the first workshop created by TIPP, and in fact began before the organisation itself. Pump! on the other hand was designed when the organisation was fully in existence.

The manuals written here are the end point of a process of collaboration and project pilots, but they do not mean to fix the programmes in stone. The fact that they are written differently and do not follow the same stylistic formula is an illustration that they are as much historical moments in the development of two pieces of work as they are polished practice manuals.

Figure 1 The TIPP Centre

Blagg! – The History

The Blagg! workshop was developed in late 1991 and early 1992 by what was soon to become the Theatre in Prisons and Probation (TIPP) Centre at Manchester University Drama Department. The workshop was a joint initiative created in partnership with Greater Manchester Probation Service. The initial aim of the project was to create a training workshop for probation clients that looked at and challenged offending behaviour. It was hoped that it would cover a variety of relevant topics such as car crime, theft, drug use and violence and that it would provide probation staff with additional material from which to develop their work. The original idea was that the creative team would devise four separate training days, on distinct topics. Each one would be run centrally in Greater Manchester and clients from across the area would be invited to what would be billed as a special event.

Whilst UK probation practice has changed significantly over the period that Blagg! has existed, the use of groupwork as a part of the probation order has remained central. When Blagg! was first planned, there were voluntary groups that individual probation officers could encourage their clients to attend. These tended to be of the 'drop in' variety, where the opportunity to meet people, have a coffee and perhaps a game of pool were offered. Occasionally they were more focused and a workshop such as Blagg! might be introduced. In addition to these groups, there were conditions attached to probation orders that required probationers to attend a group focused around certain needs or issues. These might be, for example, offending behaviour, anger management, alcohol awareness, or safer driver programmes. Again at the point of the commission, Blagg! was targeted at clients on these programmes as well. Since 1992, these have become more and more structured with an increasing strict adherence to the principles of effectiveness from the 'what works' debates (see Introduction). In the late 1990s, national benchmarks for effectiveness in probation practice provide a new arena for the Blagg! workshop to find its place. The publication of *Evidence Based Practice* by Her Majesty's Inspectorate of Probation in 1998 (Chapman and Hough) showed that the 'what works' movement had come full circle with official recognition of certain groupwork programmes. This publication makes a clear commitment to drama when it states:

> Drama…if purposefully and carefully designed and delivered, can address a range of criminogenic needs including:
>
> - anti-social attitudes, beliefs and values…
> - cognitive and interpersonal skills…
> - a sense of achievement and community integration… (Chapman and Hough 1998, p.15)

From the outset of the Blagg! devising process, we were clear that it would not only be drama based but that it should also involve a design component. We wanted a 'set' in the theatrical sense, but were unsure exactly what this would be. This was a torturous demand even on the superb skills of the designer who worked with us, Jocelyn Meall. We were asking her to design a project for which there was no script, nor was there a clear precedent. The TIPP team was made up of myself and the drama lecturer, Paul Heritage. I had been working with drama in probation centres for two years and Paul, at the time, was working extensively in prisons, particularly in HMP Manchester (Strangeways). We both knew that the various institutional spaces in which we worked needed altering by not only changing the activity within them, but also by bringing in

Figure 2 The Blagg! set

new colours and objects. If our agenda was one of change, even in the restricted agenda of personal change demanded by offending behaviour programmes, the environment also needed shifting. To this end the eventual Blagg! set was designed and built. This manual is written assuming that the set is not being used and a simple chalkboard and flip chart are available. Whilst the set does add to the Blagg! experience, the workshop does work without it. Please contact the TIPP Centre for more information about the props.

The development process involved the creative team – Paul Heritage and myself from the TIPP Centre, and Jocelyn Meall as designer – bringing ideas back to a 'Liaison Committee' of probation officers. They responded to the initial proposals, offering their own thoughts and expertise. A probation perspective continually informed the development of the project so that the final product would be relevant and appropriate for existing practice. From the perspective of the Liaison Committee, we were looking to design a programme that enhanced and complemented existing activity. This was a process of simultaneous research and practice over many months. The workshop never stood still: new approaches from offending behaviour programmes were constantly stood on their feet to be reinvented and reworked. Defining which offences to concentrate on took a long time. Turning the 'flip chart and pen approach' of much groupwork into something more dynamic took even longer. The single most significant development in this process happened during a difficult practical exploration workshop. We had become utterly stuck and the ideas for the workshops were increasingly confused, complicated and convoluted. We decided to return to the practice that had already been developed in probation centres – on a non-offending behaviour brief – and examine its structure. The workshops in these situations relied heavily on the development of very simple narratives. This became the key to the problem. To involve people in a participatory process, first the structure needed simplicity and clarity. This was not so that the ideas or the concerns were simplified, but so that the process itself was not mystifying. The exercises we had started to develop were becoming so elaborate, that sessions would have become a struggle of definition and explanation rather than an open process of practical debate. Second, we realised that we should have trusted in our theatre skills from the outset, rather than rely too heavily on the offending behaviour programmes that were already in existence. Working in the frame of 'character and plot', we then moved from explicitly developing an offending behaviour workshop to creating a 'play making kit'. By using a workshop structure that asked for a character, asked what they did, asked what were the consequences of what they did and ask why it happened in the first place, we were following a very basic narrative, that simultaneously involved exploration of key behavioural moments. Creating a story allowed us to examine offences and offending.

This basic narrative structure is the core to Blagg! Once discovered, the various exercises that now make up the whole of this manual were gradually grafted on. Some were implicit from the outset and some evolved from running the workshop itself. The simplicity of the structure also allowed us to abandon our search for separate workshops for each issue. Blagg! was to evolve into a general format into which each group could place their issues. The structure became the method by which those issues were to be explored. It was at this time that the name Blagg! was first chosen. The word has its origins in the French word 'blague' which means humbug or claptrap. Its current usage in the UK is widespread, but when we were first devising the workshop, it was a particularly popular word amongst probation clients. To blag somebody meant to deceive them, to pull the wool over their eyes. It meant to convince somebody of something that was not necessarily true. A blagger was a booster, a sweet talker; a person who could wrap you around their finger with clever excuses for their actions. A blag however was also a very specific word for a crime. An 'armed blag' in the north west of England and perhaps elsewhere is an armed robbery. 'Blag' was thus a word that was directly linked to offending, but also linked to a notion of performance; blagging was acting. The skills that many probation clients and prisoners admired in the 'good blagger' were the skills we were using and working with in the Blagg! workshop. It became the ideal name and allowed us an easy way in, when explaining the workshop to new participants. The second 'g' was added because, as is explained in the manual, the central character of the workshop is 'Jo Blaggs' – a play on the everyperson Jo Bloggs.

The Blagg! workshop was piloted at two national conferences,[1] at a Greater Manchester Probation staff familiarisation training day, and four days with Greater Manchester clients. These first 'outings' allowed us to assess the impact of the workshop, the ease with which games and exercises were used and the degree to which clients and probation staff felt the workshop was relevant or helpful. The feedback and comments were then absorbed over a period of time into the overall structure and delivery style of the workshop. One of the key points realised at this stage was that it was very difficult to run centrally organised days for the probation service. Blagg! was seen as more effective

---

[1]   A National Association for the Care and Resettlement of Offenders (NACRO) conference in 1992, and the Acting for a Change: Theatre with Offenders conference in the same year at Manchester University.

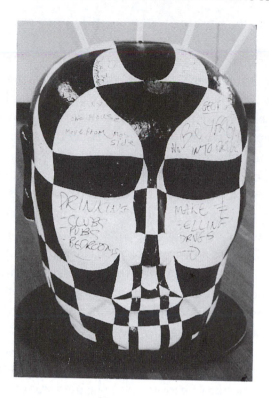

Figure 3 Jo Blaggs

when used in local probation centres with clients on existing programmes. Blagg! was very soon 'on tour'.

One of the objectives in designing Blagg! was that it could be run by non-drama specialists. Following from the logic of the title of Boal's book *Games for Actors and Non-Actors* (1992), the workshop did not only have non-actors in mind as the participants, but in the long term it also had non-directors in mind as the facilitators. For a true integration of the methodology, external staff could not be continually relied upon to be running groupwork sessions. In principle, of course, this appears appropriate, but in fact this has continued to generate debate amongst theatre practitioners and probation staff. Many probation officers still feel that the external theatre facilitator can provide a valuable shift in emphasis for the client group and can therefore create an impact, one which a familiar probation officer would not be able to do. Similarly, some theatre facilitators will comment on an almost intuitive sense of the theatre process that they have when developing the Blagg! workshop, which is impossible to pass on in a staff training course. Whilst I have sympathies with both these views, it is a source of pride that Blagg! is run by non-theatre staff in many contexts. Each staff member brings his or her style and strengths to the delivery of the workshop. Theatre processes are beginning to be viewed as a vital part of groupwork. They are a relevant and important part of the daily practice, and not a grafted extra.

Since 1992, the Blagg! workshop has been adapted and used in a variety of probation and prison settings. The TIPP Centre has travelled across the UK and internationally, using and demonstrating the workshop for prisons, probation centres, young offender institutions and young people's groups. There are nine organisations that have the set and staff trained to use it. These include three adult men's prisons, one women's prison, two Young Offender Institutions, two probation services and one drugs action team. The workshop is used as a one-off activity to provoke discussions and thought, or it is used as part of ongoing groupwork programmes. Some areas use it as the first session of a course to introduce themes that will be dealt with in greater detail later, others use it as the final session, as a means to wrap up the programme. It becomes a means to both consolidate and practise what has been learnt. Still others use it as an assessment mechanism, through which individuals can be referred onto other relevant programmes. It has been part of compulsory attendance court-ordered programmes and also as a voluntary activity. The workshop has dealt with almost every crime imaginable – from theft to violence, drugs to drunken driving, and chequebook fraud to arson. Increasingly, it has not only been strictly crime that is placed at the centre of the workshop. In its use with younger people, Blagg! has concentrated on incidents such as 'the reason a person got expelled', 'the moment that lead to an individual being suspended', or 'why a character was grounded by her/his parents'. Blagg! now explores crises, situations of conflict, the breaking of rules, wherever they may arise and almost in any context.

I am keen that Blagg! is used in as wide a variety of settings as is possible. Only staff and participants from these places can decide whether the workshop is relevant. We of course would be pleased to hear how and where it has been used.

Good luck and welcome to the art of blagging!

The Blagg! Manual

INTRODUCTION

Welcome to the Blagg! manual. Within these pages is a blow-by-blow account of all you should need to run a Blagg! workshop. Each exercise is described in full and any problems that may arise when they are being put into practice, are discussed.

The manual should be used as a guide to the workshop rather than a strict plan. Although it does follow a logical order, you will often find yourself deviating because of the material the group comes up with. This is to be encouraged – as long as the group does not deviate to the extent that you are no longer dealing with anything relevant to the workshop! Groupwork is organised differently depending on the context and the needs of the group. Using Blagg! should adapt to these constraints.

This manual can also be used outside the context of a Blagg! workshop. The exercises can be adapted and organised as starting points for discussions, debates, and role plays on a variety of issues.

Blagg! is made up of a series of exercises that have been designed specifically for the purpose of the workshop. They do not claim to be magical solutions to very complex problems, rather they aim to be accessible techniques for use by staff engaged in groupwork. Any person who has experience of either running groups, teaching or using drama will not find them difficult. As an approach to dealing with offending or problem behaviour, Blagg! seeks to re-work traditional methodologies into a practical drama-based format. The research into the workshop, concentrated both on existing groupwork practice and also on current educational, social and therapeutic uses of drama.

TYPE AND SIZE OF GROUP

Blagg! was originally commissioned for groups of up to twenty people. Different organisations have varying average group sizes. A classroom may have this many, but a probation group will have far less people. Whilst an optimum may be approximately ten participants, it has been run with as many as the originally intended twenty and as few as three. The numbers change the style and impact of the workshop. The smaller the group, the more intense the experience. Also the smaller the group, the quicker the workshop goes!

Blagg! has been run with diverse groups: young and old, prisoners with very serious offences or young people who are struggling at school. It has been run with men-only groups, women-only groups and with mixed groups. Each group changes the event and will make their own connections with the material. A Blagg! can be very serious and contemplative or it can be a highly entertaining experience. There is no one way. Each group, its composition and its objectives will effect the type of Blagg! workshop that takes place. A Blagg! with a homogeneous group looking at a pre-arranged topic of course will be more focused, than a group made up of clients from different probation settings. Positive work can be done, however, with such groups. Single sex groups can offer a clarity of purpose, but a mixed group can sometimes be richer in offering a greater variety of perspectives.

It is important that Blagg! is run by at least two people. One may take a lead on the facilitation and the other may be a co-worker. This might be someone who is part of your team, or a member of staff from the agency in which you are a guest. It is always valuable to have someone who is participating as a group member, as they will pick up contributions from the group that are easily missed and they can also play the role of a keen participant/volunteer to smooth the running of aspects of the workshop.

SPACE AND THE SET

The Blagg! workshop needs space enough for people to move around relatively freely. It has been run in the space of a double cell (small) and within a prison gymnasium (cavernous). Large spaces tend to make concentration very difficult and also allow people to get lost around the edges. Somewhat of a squash is always better than a huge expanse because concentration is easier, and people are more likely to contribute.

Whilst Blagg! was originally designed with a large colourful set, it is not vital for the running of the workshop (see Figure 4). If you are interested in the set please contact the TIPP Centre. The original set consists of:

- Chequered fibreglass 'Jo Blaggs' head
- Explosion floor cloth
- Thought bubbles on dowels and bases
- White lino squares
- Yellow lino arrows

- Time scale playing cards

This manual is written as the non-set owning version. For the purposes of the workshop described here, you will need flip chart paper and pens, several newspapers, and if available, masking or insulation tape for the floor. If there is a chalkboard, this can be used for a number of the exercises. In addition, you will need a set of cards with the times written on them – one hour, one day, one week, two weeks, one month, three months, six months and one year.

Figure 4 The Blagg! workshop. Photo by Bridget Eadie

TIMINGS

The entire Blagg! workshop was originally designed for a day. However, due to the nature of much groupwork practice it is more often run in two-hour sessions. A full Blagg! can be completed in two such sessions. This would mean a fairly rapid pace, however this is positive for concentration and keeping a group participating and engaged. It is important that the workshop is adapted to the timetable of the institution that is using it. The work that develops from a Blagg! can be incorporated into many more sessions than just the first two.

This manual does not offer detailed timings for each section or exercise. This is because they would depend on too many variables for them to be useful. The size of the group and their enthusiasm can radically change timings.

USING THIS MANUAL

Whilst the TIPP Centre has always provided training with Blagg! workshops, this manual should enable staff to start running the workshop themselves. It is important that the exercises are perhaps tried out between staff before they are done with a client group for the first time. Alternatively they can be used openly with a group, explaining that this is a trial run and you are looking for feedback on the workshop process itself. One of the principles of this area of work is that simply by reading you will learn very little. You must get up and 'do'!

THE EXERCISES

As stated already all the exercises outlined below are to be used flexibly. The user may at first take the exercises they are comfortable with and run them for the specific issues they are addressing in their work. However they should not be chosen at random. The Blagg! workshop has been designed to cover different elements of offending/rule breaking/conflict in a relatively logical order. Sometimes you might find it difficult to use one exercise if another has not been completed first.

STARTING OFF

If you are running the first session of a course, ground rules will need to be set up. These will vary depending on the organisation or institution. If the Blagg! takes place in the middle of a course that you have been invited into, it is important to check the ground rules that have already been established. Ground rules usually cover anti-discriminatory behaviour and language and expectations on group members in terms of participation. Whilst there may be pre-arranged groupwork ground rules for an institution, it is always valuable to negotiate ground rules so that they are owned by all.

DESCRIBING BLAGG!

Many groups will understandably be very anxious about the term 'drama'. Images of stressful moments at school pretending to be a tree dominate the popular imagination. These need to be countered and dispelled. This workshop will not be asking the participants to be trees! It is important that the group are not put off before the work starts. Blagg! can be introduced as a three-dimensional board game involving some role play rather than a drama workshop. This is not dishonest as it actually informs the group about the nature of the work better than the phrase 'drama workshop'. It can also be referred to as participatory or interactive groupwork. If, however, you are working in a context where the participants are expecting a drama workshop then of course it should be introduced as one. The important thing is to minimise any anxiety the group might have at the start. The word 'blag' itself should also be explained if it is not familiar. If you think this might confuse your group, you could call the workshop something else altogether. If the word is familiar, the group should be asked what they understand by the term and why they think the workshop has been called this.

PART 1

1. Warm-ups

WHAT?

Group games (warm-ups or icebreakers) involving action, participation, and a degree of both competition and co-operation. The first step to standing up in front of the group. Two games are outlined here. There are of course many more and you may wish to use your own. The number used depends on the time you have for the session and the degree to which you feel the group needs warming up.

WHY?

These games relax a group, lighten the atmosphere, and energise often very tired or low energy individuals. They aim to reduce immediately any anxiety about the subsequent work, bring the group together in a joint activity and aid concentration. It is important from the outset that the group realise that this workshop aims to engage not just their mind but their whole body.

HOW?

★ EXERCISE 1: FRUIT BOWL

1   The group needs to sit on chairs in a fairly wide circle. Remove your own chair and stand up, leaving one chair fewer than there are group members.

2   Introduce the fact that you are going to play a quick warm-up and without explaining the rest of the game, go round the circle giving each person a fruit name – apple, orange and pear. Include yourself in this.

3   Explain the rules. A person comes to the centre of the circle and says a fruit name, if it is yours, you must get up and find a new seat. The person who is stood in the circle must try to sit as well. This leaves a different person standing in the middle. They then repeat the process.

4   Rather than saying a single fruit, the person in the middle can say 'Fruit Bowl', at which everyone changes chairs.

5   Change the rules in the middle of the game, adding that people are not allowed to move (shuffle) to the seat next to them. They must cross the circle.

Notes

- Doing a game is always easier than explaining it. Keep descriptions to a minimum and get going. If someone has not quite got the gist of it, they will pick it up once the game starts.

- Beware of flying chairs and play-fighting to gain seats. A warning of this can be given at the beginning.

- Change the names of the fruit if appropriate (i.e. non-European fruits). Also change the words altogether to make them relevant to the topic which you might be discussing (i.e. Lawyer, Judge, Defendant!).

Trouble shooting

- *Small numbers*...cut the number of fruits down to two. With very small groups this exercise cannot be played.

- *Apathy*...this game does not tell individuals to get up and run around. People do it because it is part of a game structure. It is very good at getting the apathetic moving. If someone is not moving on each go, persuade him or her to participate by using the conventions set out by the game (i.e. 'you're cheating!' 'I thought that was the chair you were on before', etc.) rather than the wider rules of the group (i.e. 'Join in like everyone else', 'Come on – participate'). This technique is basically pointing out what someone *is* doing, rather than what they are not doing (i.e. they *are* cheating rather than they *are not* taking part). Telling someone they are cheating should always be done with a smile – it is not a very serious offence. By emphasising the active – the cheating – however inactive it may seem, you are giving them little opportunity to opt out. Your language is including them rather than excluding them. This is a technique vital in all the exercises outlined in this manual.

★ EXERCISE 2: ISLANDS

1   Place the sheets of a newspaper around the floor. You should put out less than one per participant.

2   Ask the group to walk around the room, taking care not to tread on the sheets. They can be described as 'islands'.

3   When you shout 'Go!' each participant should get on his or her nearest sheet. You are allowed more than one person per piece of paper. A person is on a sheet if no part of their body is touching the surrounding floor. 'Go' can be replaced with 'sharks' if you are using the island metaphor.

4   When successfully completed, ask the group to move about the room again. As they do this, remove one or half a sheet and repeat the process.

5   Keep repeating this. As it gradually gets harder, indicate to the group that they should spend more time thinking about *how* they are going to get all the group members on the remaining 'islands'.

4   End the game when the whole group has successfully negotiated getting on one or two remaining pieces of newspaper… or when then have collapsed in an amicable pile.

5   Ask for feedback on the exercise from the group. What did they like about it? What happened by the end? Why was this exercise used? and what might it have to do with the subject matter of the group?

Notes

- Do not make the exercise too hard. If you have a large number of participants allow for more 'islands' at the end.

- This game is specifically designed to break down barriers around touch. This can be particularly appropriate for men's groups, but a facilitator must be aware of, and be sensitive to, the problems this might pose for mixed gender groups and for individuals with different cultural backgrounds/expectations.

- Use of the metaphor of 'islands' and 'sharks' can depend on whether you feel the group will view this as too childish or not. Ironically, this may be more of a problem for an adolescent group than an adult group.

- The end questions should always be open. Questioning is a vital part of the workshop and should be drawing analysis of the experiences from the group themselves rather than imposing pre-set meanings.

Trouble shooting

- *Hovering*…some individuals will walk around a single 'island' or drag it along with their feet. It should be jokingly pointed out rather than prohibited.

- *Over enthusiasm*…People can dive on the 'islands' which is okay when there are plenty to go around, but it must be avoided as the game progresses. Emphasise the need for participants to work out together how they are all going to balance safely. Rather than shouting 'Go!' towards the end, you can give a calmer instruction so they think before they jump.

- *Victimisation*…The potential for this needs to be recognised in all exercises and conscious effort is needed to avoid it. Facilitators must be aware how an exercise could be used by some to intimidate other group members. In this exercise one person may continually be left on their own. The co-worker should recognise this and make an effort to join that person. The game, however, will eventually overcome this because individuals have to join together by the end.

2. How to Play

WHAT?

This section offers an introduction to the techniques which individuals need to be familiar with, in order to participate fully in a Blagg! workshop. It explains the rules of the game and indicates how the role plays are to be set up. Participants will be eased into tableaux work (still pictures out of bodies), and start to develop simple improvisation. You may decide to do only one of the tableaux exercises and one of the tableaux into role play exercises.

WHY?

Before any game/exercise is done, it is necessary to know and practise the techniques needed to successfully accomplish it. With football you practise your skills before you start a game. Similarly with Blagg! participants should be put at ease by a brief demonstration of what they will be doing. This aims to dispel any fear they have about taking part.

In addition these opening exercises set the tone for the workshop and make some key points about participation and the art of looking which are vital to groupwork. This section introduces the idea that if group members are not in the acting area, they, as audience, will still have a significant role to play. They will be expected to participate from their seat. Also theatre is about looking closely, reading what is happening in front of them – reflecting on action. This reflection on action is a key skill to be developed throughout Blagg! and is introduced here.

HOW?

★ **EXERCISE 1: PAIRED TABLEAUX[1]**

1 Ask each person in the room to find a partner. Explain that you are going to demonstrate how the workshop is 'played'.

2 Get each pair to label themselves A and B. State that A is a sculptor and B is a lump of clay. Explain that A is going to sculpt B in to a statue.

3 Take one member of the group – a willing volunteer – and demonstrate how to sculpt. You do this by moving each part of their body gently into the place that you want it for the picture. This can be very detailed, with each finger being moved to its exact position. Mention that faces are hard to mould and therefore sculptors are allowed to pull an expression for their clay to copy. Other than this the clay can do no work.

4 Ask for sculpting to be done in complete silence. Clay cannot talk!

5 Depending on the time, offer a number of progressively more difficult things for them to sculpt. You may start by asking them to create whatever they want. Something abstract or concrete. If you are concerned with lack of participation, offer them fixed ideas such as 'teacher' or 'footballer' (characters they are familiar with) – and then move to the less concrete – 'fear', 'victory' and so forth.

6 When each sculptor is happy with a piece of work ask him or her to move around the room looking at the other exhibits. Do this after each new sculpt. Ask questions to get the group reading the images. What do they all have in common? What do people like about each example? If the group have created images which you did not give a title, ask the group (before you ask the sculptor) what they see. What titles could be given? You are looking for multiple readings, not for fixed or 'correct' readings.

7 Swap clay and sculptor (A and B) after each exhibition.

---

[1]   'Paired tableaux' is an exercise very much based on the Image Theatre of Augusto Boal. See *Games for Actors and Non-Actors* (Boal 1992).

Notes

- If your group are anxious about touching each other for whatever reason, run the same exercise but add that sculptors cannot touch their clay, they can only usher or conduct it into position. This resembles a miniature version of someone bringing a landing plane to the right place on a runway.

- Try and get the group to be as precise as possible. Move fingers, check feet position, and tilt heads. Sculpting is a fine art.

- Accept all readings. One of the key purposes of this form of groupwork is to develop an individual's capacity to see and then see again. Everybody's subjective reading can be appropriate and diversity of interpretation must be championed.

Trouble shooting

- *Noisy pairs…* If two people are good friends and happy to disrupt they can easily do so in this exercise. Try to anticipate this and get staff to partner the more difficult. Keep telling them clay cannot talk!

- *Moving exhibits…* Holding a pose can be difficult. Encourage the clay to remain still but also keep up the momentum of the exercise. If one pair are have finished rapidly do not be afraid to give them the next thing to sculpt. If one 'exhibit' is being looked at for quite a time by the group, give them an opportunity to relax and 'shake out' before re-taking their pose.

★ **EXERCISE 2: WHAT'S THE STORY?**

1   If you have not used Exercise 1, explain that you are demonstrating how Blagg! is to be played. Say that it is very simple and ask for two volunteers. If you do 'What's the story?' after the first exercise, take one of the existing pairs.

2   Ask the first volunteer to stand facing the rest of the group and the second to stand behind but to one side of the first, at the other side of the room. There should be at least five strides between them. A member of the group watching directly in front of the first volunteer should be able to see the second clearly.

3   Ask the group the open question 'What do you see?' This should get the simple replies of 'two people standing there' etc. Develop this by asking 'what's the story?' You are asking them what would they would think was going on if they saw two people standing like this.

4   Accept all replies – however ridiculous, or obstructive they might seem. Go round the whole group asking for different individual's impressions.

5   When this is exhausted, ask the volunteer furthest away to take one step forward and repeat numbers 3 and 4.

6   Repeat the above process until the furthest volunteer has walked past the person in the front. Ask the group for their impressions of the exercise.

7   Ask the group for their favourite interpretation.

8   Take the volunteers back to the places they held for that interpretation and ask those watching for a line of dialogue for each. 'What are they about to say?' Make sure the volunteers have heard their line.

9   Tell the group that you are about to bring the scene to life, that the acting will be fantastic and therefore they must give a huge round of applause when it is finished. Count to three or on a handclap bring the scene to life. The volunteers should say their single lines and then receive the rapturous applause!

10   Tell the group that the acting/role play in Blagg! is rarely going to be any harder than that.

11   This exercise can be repeated with different original positions. For example, one person standing behind another seated on a chair.

Notes

- You can combine Exercise 1 with Exercise 2 by doing the 'What's the story?' on pairs of exhibits. You do not have to do all these first exercises however. Run the ones with which you feel most comfortable or the ones for which you have enough time.

- If you have a shorter workshop cut out steps 5 and 6. Choose from the interpretations given to the first position.

- If the group does not understand what you mean by 'What's the story?', you can preface it by saying something like: 'If you saw this at the beginning of a film…', 'If you saw two people standing like this where you live…' etc.

- Get the lines of dialogue to be exact as possible. 'Have you got a light?' rather than 'He's asking him for a light'. The group are the directors, the volunteers should not have to do any work.

- Make the beginning and end of the scene as clear as possible. This will set up the conventions for the rest of the workshop.

- This exercise can act as a barometer or litmus test for your group. If every interpretation is related to violence or potential violence, it gives you a strong clue as to the group's concerns. If all the interpretations are about interpersonal or relationship conflicts, you then have further evidence of what your group want to cover.

- Both Exercises 1 and 2 are crucial for introducing the difference between 'fact' and 'opinion'. Each reading of the image is a personal interpretation of reality – an opinion. This differentiation should be taken as a theme through the workshop as a whole. This is particularly important in offending behaviour work, where groups will tend to view their opinion as 'correct' and others as misguided and wrong. Encouraging multiple readings is the first stage towards work on perspective taking, decision making and victim empathy. All opening exercises should be referred back to during the rest of the workshop to illustrate these points when necessary.

Trouble shooting

- *Volunteering*…can often prove problematic. Asking for a volunteer can undo the good work already done on building the commitment and the energy of the group. It can act to puncture the atmosphere. One option is to say that the volunteers have to do less work than the people watching. This appeals to participants' apathetic side but nearly always works! Another way is to simply take someone by the arm as you ask for a volunteer. This usually takes group members by surprise but they do respond positively.

- *Being crude*…is usually done to test facilitators out. If someone suggests the still picture is something very rude, repeat it, say it could be and suggest that the person who offered the interpretation is clearly demonstrating a willingness to volunteer to act it out for the group. This usually delineates what is acceptable pretty quickly! If they are being offensive, a contribution should be restated in more appropriate language. Situations like this are open for interpretation by groupworkers and will also be subject to the ground rules that have been established and agreed upon by the group.

★ EXERCISE 3: ARGUMENTS

1   Following from 'What's the story?' tell the group that the next exercise, rather than creating a scene from nothing, starts with a simple idea: an argument.

2   Ask the group for examples of different arguments – 'Who is involved?', 'Where did they take place?', 'Over what?', etc.

3   Take two volunteers and ask the group to position them (sculpt them) as though they were in the argument of their choice. The group can either tell them where to stand or come up and physically position them.

4   Ask for a line for each character.

5   Count to three or on a handclap bring the scene to life. As with 'What's the story?', end with loud applause.

6   Comment on how good the acting was and on how easy people are finding it!

Notes

- Sometimes the arguments can continue of their own accord. This should be encouraged as it further demonstrates how Blagg! will be run. Use the applause to stop them when you think appropriate.

- Try to make the original argument picture as precise as possible. Ask the group questions to finalise it. What would his face look like? How would s/he be holding her or his hands? Does that say argument to you? Invite changes until the whole group is happy.

Trouble shooting

- *Over-enthusiasm*…Arguments can quickly disintegrate into violence. The facilitator must maintain control at all times. Use the applause as a way of preventing the argument from going too far. Loud clapping will snap actors out of any scene. It can be pointed out to the group that in drama the interesting thing is why a fight happened, not the fight itself. If the group deems a violent reaction to the argument likely, it offers the perfect opportunity to introduce a ground rule about violence during role play. This could either be that if a participant thinks their character would act violently to a particular incident, they should step out of the scene and say so – 'I would hit him now' etc. Alternatively, the rule can be that when you say 'freeze', the actors do exactly that. If the group responds violently to a number of incidents, this becomes vital material to examine during the session.[2]

2   It must be emphasised that in many years of running Blagg!, I have never had a role play disintegrate into violence in any way.

★ **EXERCISE 4: THE INTERVIEW**

1   As the argument above but with the title 'Interview'. Change the setting of the interview depending on the group with whom you are working. Police interview, interview with school authorities and so forth. This exercise offers a chance to bring in more than two people and for most clients/inmates/young people it should be very familiar territory.

Notes

- The dialogue almost always needs to be extended beyond the first few lines.

- Participants will often try to get the scene exactly right. This might involve lengthy debates about police/school procedure. Try and fast-forward the interview to where the central topic is being discussed.

The 'How to play' section should conclude with a summary of what has been demonstrated. Briefly, Blagg! is played by first creating still pictures, giving them a script and then bringing them to life. The audience – those sitting around the edge of the circle watching – will need to be as active in this process as those on their feet. Once people in the group have successfully negotiated this introduction, they will have no problems with the rest of the workshop.

Figure 5 James Thompson 'blagging'. Photo: The TIPP Centre

3 Who is Jo Blaggs?

WHAT?

The Blagg! workshop concentrates on one fictitious individual named Jo Blaggs. It is this person that the group will then follow through the rest of the workshop. This section is the moment when the group collectively creates the character with whom they will work for the whole of the workshop.

WHY?

On a self-contained workshop, it is vital all are involved and drawn in as much as possible. The Jo Blaggs character acts as a focus for the work to be done, and avoids dealing with one individual's case history directly. Clearly individuals' experiences are brought in, but the fictional character leaves this at a safe distance. The workshop's objective – to sort Jo's life out – can resonate directly with a group member, but at the same time demonstrates the abilities they have to deal collectively with problems or difficult situations. The name Jo has been specifically chosen to be both male and female. Staff or the group, however, could change it altogether if they felt it was inappropriate.

HOW?

★ EXERCISE: WHO IS JO BLAGGS?

1   Draw a large head on a piece of flip chart paper or on a chalkboard. Alternatively, ask a group member to do it for you. This is Jo Blaggs! Explain that for the workshop to succeed you need a character and it is the group's job to create that character.

2   Start the questioning by placing Jo in their context, making him/her familiar to the group. For example 'Jo is a member of this group…' or 'Jo is on probation…', or 'Jo is a person who was meant to be here but could not make it today…'.

3   The following is a guide to questions building from those mentioned above. This list should help you to develop a useable Jo character. You can add more or cut it short, depending on the time available. This section takes on its own momentum, but it is worth having some key areas covered. Encourage the group to ask their own questions. You need to find out the following information:

  • Is Jo male or female?

  • How old is s/he?

  • Where does Jo live?

  • Who, if anybody, does Jo live with?

  • Family? Does Jo see them? Does Jo like them? Do they like Jo?

- What are Jo's interests?
- What are Jo's ambitions?

As each answer is given, more detail can be asked for.

- She lives in Manchester – where exactly?
- He likes music – what type?

4   Write all replies on the 'head', covering it with as much detail as possible.

5   This exercise ends when a fairly but not fully rounded character has been developed. Any gaps can be filled in later in the workshop.

Notes

- It is vital that Jo be similar to the group. There is no point in a group of young men working on a sixty-year-old woman for example.
- If helpful, a participant can do the writing whilst the facilitator asks the questions. Ensure that this will not cause embarrassment with literacy. Alternatively a co-worker can do it.
- Constantly recap the replies already given as the questioning continues. This helps build up and clarify a picture of the person being created. It is also a good way of memorising character details and avoiding an over-reliance on the reading skills of the group.

Trouble shooting

- *Contradictory answers*…When one participant insists Jo is nineteen and another wants them to be twenty-five you can do two things. First, you could compromise – ask for a middle figure. Or you could ask the rest of the group what would be the most realistic age for someone who could be part of that group. This debate, and the skills the group have to use to reach consensus, are a vital part of the groupwork. It should not be regarded as a problem, but as a necessary part of the process.

- *Wildly inappropriate answers*…Sabotage is common, take it in your stride! The first strategy can be to check with the rest of the group whether the characteristic mentioned is realistic. The key is that Jo must be someone who could be part of this group. This often scuppers it at the first hurdle. Your second option is to remind the group that they will be acting this character and anything they suggest they will have to perform. This can often frighten them off the more ridiculous replies. What is 'inappropriate' is of course for you to decide, considering ground rules and anti-discriminatory practice. For example, I would be very suspicious of an all white group creating a black Jo Blaggs, although in my experience it has never happened. You need to be aware without being censorious.

4 What has s/he done?

WHAT?

Finding out the moment the rest of the workshop will concentrate on – one of Jo Blaggs' offences. An offence can be a infringement of the law, a breaking of a school rule, a disciplinary issue in the home or any action that might be viewed as having negative consequences.

WHY?

Blagg! focuses on one offence in order that all the reasons for it and consequences of it are demonstrated. One primary aim is to show that even the most minor of incidents has a multitude of repercussions for the perpetrator and for others. When dealing with a typical Jo Blaggs incident, issues relevant to a variety of different behaviour patterns always arise.

HOW?

★ THE EXERCISE: WHAT HAS S/HE DONE?

1   This and the following exercises are done in the middle of the circle of chairs. If possible, you should create concentric circles with tape on the floor – a target or ripple effect – to indicate the acting area.

2   Tell the group that you need to know what Jo has done for the purpose of the workshop and that you want someone to show in a still picture, the precise moment of the incident. Jo breaking the car window, hitting the person, stealing the money – not before or after. At this stage you are just looking for Jo by him or herself.

3   Get the one volunteer to stand at the centre of the circle. Ask the group whether it is clear what s/he is doing and whether they want to change him/her in any way.

4   Change the volunteer either by people going up and physically moving him/her, by verbal suggestion or by someone replacing them altogether.

5   Do this until the group is happy with their image. Check this by asking whether they recognise what the volunteer is doing – 'Does this say car crime to you?' etc.

Notes

• Usually the most likely crime becomes clear from the character creation section. If not, a consensus has to be reached. Several tableaux can be done to keep this a practical exploration rather than a discussion.

- Participants will often respond with a laugh of recognition when someone gets an image exactly right. Use this as an indication of when to agree on a tableau.

Trouble shooting

- *Keeping the image still*…People find it very hard to stay still for any length of time. This section must move with energy otherwise a volunteer is going to sit down or finish off the crime! Avoid drawn-out debates.

5 What is Jo thinking?

WHAT?

The section aims to discover what is going on in Jo's head at the moment of the crime, translating these into Jo's feelings and ordering them in terms of which is the most and which is the least dominant. It also seeks to stimulate debate amongst the group about the differences between thoughts and feelings and how they feel when they are offending.

WHY?

This is done to find clues about Jo's motivation for offending. The exercise and the debate should build further the connection between the fictitious Jo and the participants in the group, as well as being a useful discussion in its own

Figure 6 Jo Blaggs' feelings. Photo: The TIPP Centre

right. The exercise also provides a useful benchmark for later reference and comparison.

Developing group members' understanding and awareness of the thinking and the feelings behind actions is an important part of all offending behaviour groupwork. It aims to replace the 'it just happened' belief, with an acknowledgement that action is based on a person's thoughts and feelings.

HOW?

★ THE EXERCISE: WHAT IS JO THINKING?

1   Ask the group to all stand up and copy the still image which the one volunteer should still be doing from the previous exercise.

2   Tell them that they are all now Jo and about to commit the offence.

3   Say that after a count of three you want them all to say out aloud what they think Jo would be thinking at this moment.

4   Pause.

5   Count to three, listen to the sound of the responses and ask them all to sit down.

6   Once seated you can comment on how the thoughts sounded – were they loud, angry, energetic, etc.? Then ask each individual in turn what they said.

7   Focus a discussion on these replies by saying they need to be translated into single words or feelings. Draw 'thought bubbles' on the flip chart or chalkboard and say that they need to be filled in. This process should produce useful personal comments and group debate. At first the list might be extensive, but through discussion you have to narrow it down because you will have only drawn five or six thought bubbles. For example:

    • Of the twelve you have listed, which six are the most realistic?

    • Can s/he be both afraid and excited?

    • What is the difference between fear and anxiety?

    • You might not be scared when you do this, but do you think Jo would be?

8   Once the bubbles are filled they need to be placed around the head. If they were drawn on flip chart paper, they could be cut out and placed on the original picture of the head. If the head were drawn on a chalkboard, the thought bubbles could be drawn next to the picture, then filled in. Which feeling should be at the front of the

head and which at the back – which is the strongest feeling? A debate developing from the previous discussion will start.

9   Once all the bubbles are filled in, recap progress so far. The group now know who their Jo is, they know what s/he has done and now they know what s/he was feeling at the time.

Notes

- It is important to add a sense of tension to this exercise. This can be done by altering your tone of voice. Each person *is* Jo, and they are about to commit this offence. As they express the thought, it should break the tension. This helps to identify the character Jo directly with each individual participant. They do this personally when they are standing, and then often offer their own experiences in the subsequent debate. The Jo character allows this to remain at a safe distance.

- The ideas for thoughts and feelings might be contradictory. This is fine because this is not what a real character is thinking and feeling, but what all the group think someone like that could be thinking. It is an amalgam – Jo is an everyman/woman character.

- Let the debate flow but it does not necessarily have to finish. If any important points are not covered, record them for future reference.

Trouble shooting

- *Disagreements* ...The feelings that get placed on the head should be sorted through consensus. You want to accept all the ideas, because if someone has contributed it could be personal to them. If the majority of the group are convinced that Jo would not, for example, be scared, it is still important to write it down if it has been mentioned. These are possible feelings, not actual feelings.

6 Who is affected?

WHAT?

This section aims to complete the picture of the incident. The group have only represented Jo so far and now they must discover who else was affected by the crime. A larger tableau is created and new characters invented. The group then move on to investigate these individuals and their perspectives on Jo's offence.

WHY?

It is important to move away from the familiar territory of 'Jo the offender' and start confronting the other less well-known characters in the story. The group will have been very well acquainted with the script so far – but from now on

Blagg! should start to push in new directions. The new characters should not be marginalised but 'fleshed out' and brought to centre stage.

HOW?

★ **EXERCISE 1: COMPLETE THE PICTURE**

1   Explain the metaphor. Either Jo is standing at the centre of an explosion and it is now time to find out who else is caught up in it. Or Jo's action is a stone dropped in a pond, and the ripples now impact on other people. Only one person has been put in this picture, now it is time to complete it. What you are looking for is everyone who is affected by Jo's action.

2   As each suggestion is made, ask someone – usually the person who made the suggestion – to take on the role by standing in a position near Jo. They should strike a tableau of the character, with those watching determining its accuracy. The tableau should be what they are doing at this moment. These characters should be placed according to the effect of the explosion or ripples on them. The nearer the centre (Jo), the greater the impact the incident will have on their lives.

3   Build up the picture gradually, all the time asking for new people. Mention quite early on that it is not only the characters who are physically there that can be represented, but also those that are not present and yet are affected. A mother can be shown waiting at home for her son for example. You are basically creating the cast for the 'play'.

4   Use up nearly all the group – this of course depends on numbers. For smaller groups make sure you have all the key characters. In a car theft scenario do not have two of Jo's friends in the picture if this means no car owner for example. For larger groups extend those affected as far as you can, but always keeping extra people as observers. One of the points to be emphasised is that an incident can have a variety of often unexpected results.

5   The exercise is complete when nearly all of the group members are on their feet and one or two remain on the outside as observers.

Notes

•   Try not to have too many similar characters. For example once you have one 'passer by', you do not need loads more. One policeman/woman is enough. Emphasise or chose the unexpected where possible. If the group are missing out people you regard as key, do not be afraid to prompt by asking questions. 'Whose house are they burgling…?' This might be better coming from other staff rather than the main facilitator. The following represents an example list of characters only. It is important to emphasise that the group must discover them for themselves.

- Jo's father, mother, children etc.
- the victim, the victim's boyfriend/girlfriend
- Jo's girlfriend/boyfriend
- the victim's father, mother, children etc.
- a witness, Jo's friend/accomplice
- the police
- the person Jo sells stolen goods to
- the teacher/probation officer

- Use chairs, tables etc. to recreate cars, houses and other situations.

Trouble shooting

- *Crowds*…The whole group gets up and plays all of Jo's mates, leaving no more participants. Try to prevent this before it happens! If someone mentions a grouping that they would like to see in the picture, agree but say it will be played by one person only.

- *Non-participation*…This exercise demands action from almost the whole group. If someone really cannot budge from their chair, take the role to them. A group member lying across two chairs can miraculously become Jo Blaggs' father at home in bed. This exercise is ideal for including those that have not yet taken a role or have not been particularly active.

★ EXERCISE 2: COMPLETE THE CHARACTERS

1   There are three versions of this exercise. The one you choose is dependent upon the length of your overall Blagg! session.

Version 1 – The quickest (5 minutes)

1   Go around the tableau asking each character four questions.

- What is your name?
- What are you thinking at the moment (Jo is just about to commit the crime)?
- How do you feel?
- If you knew what Jo was doing at this moment what would you say to her/him?

2   Repeat each response so that the group can all hear and absorb the information.

3   Summarise rapidly at the end.

Version 2 – Middling (10 minutes)

1   Go around the tableau asking each person a series of questions to find out more about their character. These can be much the same as the questions used to develop the Jo Blaggs character.

2   Finish each interview with the final questions from Version 1 above.

Version 3 – The longest (up to 20 minutes)

1   Break the tableau and get everyone to sit down at one side of the room. Place a chair in front of them and ask for the first character to sit in it. Everyone will be getting up so the order does not have any great significance.

2   Start a 'Hot Seat' whereby one at a time, audience members can ask the seated character questions about themselves and they have to reply in role. The facilitator should ask the first question to 'set the tone'. Make sure the questions from Version 1 are asked.

3   Set a limit on the number of questions if necessary or stop when enough information has been elicited.

Notes

• For Versions 1 and 2, a volunteer can do the questioning instead of the facilitator if appropriate. To help this process a prop can be found to act as a microphone – roving reporter style.

• The 'Hot Seat' can be done in a circle if a seat in front of the rest of the group is too threatening.

• You are trying to develop some kind of group empathy for the characters. Try to direct the questioning so it covers areas where the effect of the crime will be at its greatest.

• If a person is very involved with their character, derole them by giving them the opportunity to ask the final question. They do this by getting up from their seat and asking the empty chair. The reply should come from another group member. This will place some distance between themselves and the role.

Trouble shooting

• *Freezing*…When a character does not know what to say. The rest of the group should be encouraged to offer possible responses. This is especially necessary when the characters are particularly unfamiliar. If someone has little to say keep the interviews short.

- *Minimisation*…Making the victim 'unbothered' about the crime. At this stage the crime has not quite happened so it is not a great problem, but signs should be observed. For example, if a car owner is said to be thinking 'I hope my car gets stolen and then I can claim insurance', this is an unsubtle attempt to minimise the effect of the incident. Although the person who says this will swear blind that this is realistic and they know someone like this etc., you can challenge it directly. Bring the rest of the group into the debate. Is this thought a common one? What would be a typical feeling? Do people really want their cars stolen? etc. If necessary, have another person play the car owner. This should not be done to exclude the minimising participant. They should be thanked for their version of a car owner, and the group should be asked if anyone else could show another version of a car owner. The second version can then be compared to the first. You want to hear a different voice. This can be done for all characters if necessary.

- *Irrelevant questioning/irrelevant answers*…There can be a tendency for participants to delve into areas of a character's life that can either be humorous, rude or unnecessary. As a facilitator you should always be conscious of the direction of the process. Let participants ask questions but if it gets out of hand, reign it back in by asking your own question which brings individuals back into focus.

7 Consequence pictures

WHAT?

This section moves from the moment of the crime to the immediate consequence. The group changes the existing tableau to see what could be both the best and worst outcomes for Jo and the other characters.

WHY?

So far the workshop has concentrated on one moment and it is now vital to develop it further – explode it outwards, or see the ripples move. You want to know 'what happened next' – moving the story on. The participants must start to examine the consequences of the incident on the protagonist and also on others. Even when the consequence for Jo is good, there are usually negative outcomes for the other characters. This is why both the best and the worst consequences are examined.

HOW?

★ THE EXERCISE: CONSEQUENCE PICTURES

1   Ask the group to recreate a tableau of the best consequence of the crime for Jo. What happened to each character? Start with Jo and work outwards including all the characters from the previous image. Literally change people's position if necessary.

2   Make any key points from the tableau you feel necessary. You can ask characters what they are feeling now. This might show that this consequence might be good for Jo but it certainly is not for others. Often individuals disappear in the best consequence (the witness is miraculously not there!). This should be noted as a dream that might be a long way from reality.

3   After a short discussion ask the group to change the image so that it becomes the worst consequence for Jo. Not the worst consequence in the long term, but one that would happen immediately. Again recreate this, concentrating on all the characters starting from Jo.

Notes

- Keep the suggestions for the new images flowing through the facilitator. There is a tendency for participants to start creating a variety of different stories at this point, and whilst this can be positive, focus needs to be maintained.

- Keep the image still for as long as possible. Again there is a tendency for the action to be taken further than is necessary at this stage.

- Look for 'drama'! In creating the worst tableau you want to find a series of interesting small images making up the whole. These will become the starting points for short scenes and therefore they have to have some potential for role play. You can suggest ideas, but often these smaller images appear on their own – the mother next to the son in hospital, the girlfriend at Jo's mother's house, Jo's father and the police, etc.

- If you have restricted time you can move straight onto the worst consequence. You can try calling this simply 'the consequence' with no qualification and see what you get. If the image is too optimistic you can always then ask for the worst!

Trouble shooting

- *Enthusiasm*…As mentioned above, it is very easy for these images to explode into life. It seems strange to be warning about over-enthusiasm, but it can mean loosing sense of the direction of the workshop. Keep in mind the purpose of the workshop without stifling the group's desire to move forward.

- *No change*…Sometimes the consequence image is confusing in terms of time. If it moves only a few minutes after the crime to when Jo is being caught by the police, the image of his/her mother and father at home (for example) might be no different. This does not matter for now as all scenes will be developed in the next section. Be very clear when fixing the picture in time though – do not have different times represented in the same image as it can cause confusion.

8 Activating the image

WHAT?

The worst consequence image is brought to life. Each of the different areas is activated and the story is followed to see the effects of the crime on these people's lives. The story is exploded in all directions to see as many repercussions as possible. It concludes by returning to Jo, to see where the incident has taken him/her in the end.

WHY?

Blagg! aims to show the multitude consequences of one incident. This section gives the participants the opportunity to discover these and act the people affected. As much as is possible in a short workshop, the intention is to develop an awareness or understanding of other people's experiences and perspectives. The act of playing a victim can be powerful for both the actor and the peer group audience.

HOW?

★ THE EXERCISE: ACTIVATING THE IMAGE – I WANT TO SEE…

1   Tell the group they are now going to bring the image to life. Add that there are rules for doing this. These are called the 'stop rules' and they exist, in order to involve the group in the development and exploration of each scenario.

2   The 'stop rules' are used as follows. Any group member, including staff and facilitator, may say or shout 'Stop!' during a scene and either:

   a   Ask a question of any of the characters.

   b   Ask any character what they are thinking.

c   If they believe the scene is unrealistic, they may direct the actors to perform in a particular way, or do something to change the action.

d   For the same reason as above, they can substitute themselves for one of the actors.

3   To bring a scene to life, ask the rest of the group first what they think is happening in the still image. Then ask them to supply each actor with their first line.

4   Activate the scene by giving a clear signal to start.

5   Some scenes come to a natural ending, others you need to stop when you think the key point has been made.

6   If the scene can have a follow-up or the story continues, direct the start of a new scene. For example, if you have had a police man/woman telling a family that their daughter has been run over, you could follow this up with the family going to the hospital. Develop the story by saying 'I want to see…', moving the narrative into areas of dramatic interest.

7   When one area has exhausted itself, move to the next leaving the central image of Jo until last. You can flit from one to another – seeing a piece from the victim's family, a dialogue between witnesses, then back to the victim, then to a police interview and so forth. You are building up the story but not necessarily moving in a straight line.

8   Develop the story of what happens to Jo up to a point when s/he 'comes to a rest'. This means a point when Jo is either by her or himself or the full consequences of the crime have been realised. The most common resting point is Jo alone in a prison/police cell, but it could be Jo back at a flat alone, sitting in the street, in the cemetery etc.

Notes

- The facilitator should use the 'stop rules' to guide the development of the story and also bring scenes to an end if they are getting out of hand, becoming confused, or struggling to find a conclusion.

- Also, use the rules to find out more information that you feel may be relevant. How is that person feeling about the incident, is she telling the truth and so forth? All can be used to stimulate discussion and add depth to the exercise. Keep the energy up during this section, moving from scene to scene at speed, constantly recapping what is going on. This will maintain the group's enthusiasm. It is important for them to be actively involved as spectators as well as when they are actors.

- The scenes 'you want to see…' do not necessarily have to be realistic. You can play around with time and the realms of possibility. For example, you could have the victim meet Jo directly, you could see Jo's Dad meet the Dad of a victim, you could have a character speaking to someone who has died – take the story wherever you feel it would be interesting and relevant.

- Even though you are maintaining an overview, be sure to encourage the group to suggest and take the narrative where they think appropriate.

- It is important for all people in the large image to be activated – even if they have a minor role.

- You can bring in characters that are not present in the large image if necessary. The appearance of an aunt, or an old friend, for example, can offer new insights to people's actions and experiences.

Trouble shooting

- *Freezing* …When the actor does not know what to say. This is perfectly acceptable and should not be criticised. It allows you to open the scene out to the rest of the group and ask what they think should be said. The stop rules work with this – ultimately someone can replace the actor if they feel too uncomfortable in a role.

- *High drama*…The story can develop into areas that are upsetting and very emotionally charged. Blagg! has created scenes where a person is told of their loved one's death for example. Do not be afraid to confront difficult realities, but maintain an acute awareness of the direction of the narrative. If the work is becoming too heavy, use the stop rules or the 'I want to see…' to redirect it. The workshop should be powerful but safe. If very emotional scenes are touched upon allow adequate time out for discussion. Always put characters into the third person when doing this, so that they are not personally identified with members of the group. Distance people from the action when necessary.

9 Jo's new thoughts and feelings

WHAT?

The group have found out who Jo is, what s/he has done, what s/he was feeling at the time, and the consequences for Jo and others. How Jo is feeling at the end of all this is now investigated. The group repeat an earlier exercise to examine Jo's new thoughts and these are then compared to the original thought bubbles. The writing on the bubbles is changed if necessary. Part 1 of Blagg! ends with an image of a number of negative feelings attached to the picture of Jo's head. This offers the starting point for Part 2.

WHY?

The group has seen how Jo was thinking at the beginning of the story and it is necessary to compare this to the thoughts afterwards. The key is to link thoughts to their consequences. For example, Jo's excitement might be seen to directly lead to feelings of anger and loneliness. The group is not only seeing the consequence of Jo's actions but also the consequences of particular ways of thinking.

The final image is purposely a negative one, in order to give the group a motivation for 'sorting Jo out' in Part 2.

HOW?

1   Complete the steps under section 5 – What is Jo Thinking? All the participants will be copying Jo 'at rest'. What is s/he thinking now?

2   Compare the new thoughts and feelings to the ones already written up. Which ones have changed and which have remained the same?

3   Cross out the old and add the new feelings. Re-organise the bubbles as the group thinks appropriate.

4   Discuss the changes.

5   Close Part 1 by recapping the whole story and indicating that after the 'break' you will be returning to find out why it all happened and how it could have been prevented.

Notes

• If your break is several days, ensure the negative feeling of Jo are not held onto by the group members. Spend time discussing the workshop and the characters. How are people there different from Jo for example? It can be useful to play a closing game to bring the energy back up. One of the games from the beginning could be used.

• Although this is an obvious place for a break, another break can easily have been taken in the middle of the exercises in Part 1.

Trouble shooting

- *Little change* …If for any reason only a few of the feelings have changed, move straight onto the discussion about where the feelings are – at the front or the back of Jo's mind. Jo never stands completely still.

PART 2

The second part of Blagg! can be completed as part of the same session, or after a refreshment or lunch break. It could also take place at the next week's session. If there is a large gap between either part it is important that 'the story so far' is recapped in detail. It should be noted that Part 2 is shorter than Part 1. In addition if there has been a break, it will be important to warm the group up again with one of the original icebreaking exercises. Often in running Blagg! the 'fruit bowl' exercise is used to introduce Part 1, and the 'island' exercise Part 2 .

1 Why did it all happen?

WHAT?

The group return in time to discover and explore moments in Jo's life that lead to the incident taking place. These can be from only hours before up to years before. The small scenarios are acted out with the main characters being left standing around the centre of the explosion/ripple effect. Using the key lines from their scenes, the characters shout at Jo whilst pushing her/him towards the middle of the explosion – the place where the crime took place. The whirlwind of Jo's life is seen in quick time.

WHY?

In order that Jo's life may be 'sorted out' by the group, they need to find the different pressures and decision moments that move him/her towards the incident. The pushing exercise is a symbolic way of condensing all the experiences into one long rush towards the incident. It demonstrates visually how Jo came to that moment, whilst audibly presenting all the thoughts in his/her head.

HOW?

★ EXERCISE 1: CHOOSE THE CARD – FIND THE SCENE

1   Explain to the group that you are now going back in time to find out how Jo came to be involved in the crime in the first place.

2   Offer the time-scale cards to one group member who should choose one and then show it to the rest of the group. It will be one hour, one day, one week, one month or six months.

3   Ask the group to suggest a moment in Jo's life that period of time ago which lead to her/him committing the offence.

4   Once the incident is agreed, take a sheet of newspaper and place it around the edge of the circle at a distance from the centre relative to its significance. Ask the group to help with this decision.

5   Ask for volunteers to act out the scene. Try and limit the numbers in these scenarios to two or three. Ask them to role play the scene on or around the newspaper sheet.

6   To help the role play, get the group to offer the first two lines, and use the 'stop rules' if necessary.

7   Finish the scene when it has become clear why it leads to the offence. Ask the group to select one line from a character that sums up the pressure on Jo. This could be for example – 'It's easy money Jo', 'You're sacked', 'Call yourself a real man' and so forth. It must be key in that it moves Jo towards, not away from, the central incident. It might have been said in the scene, or might simply be the essence of what has been said.

8   Remind the character of the line and ask them to remain on the sheet.

9   Repeat this process until a variety of scenes have been witnessed. The exact number depends on the time you have, and the numbers in the group.

10   Sometimes the group will only create scenes in which Jo is a victim of external pressure. The crime is because all these other people were making his/her life difficult. Take a new sheet of newspaper and mark it with a large question mark. Ask for a moment just before the incident or the actual time Jo made the final decision to act. Role play this with one character on the sheet only. They will say what Jo is thinking to him/herself. Their key line becomes the strongest thing Jo says to him/herself to convince him/herself that the offence is worth doing. This can be played with two people – Jo arguing with another side of him/herself – if the group finds it easier. Occasionally a group will see the necessity for this square themselves and at other times it might not be needed at all.

11 As each new person is put on a sheet, recap each character's line until finally you have a number of participants dotted around the central area.

Notes

- If two good ideas for one time period are suggested, either do both, combine them or look for a compromise.

- If there are several good suggestions for a key line combine them into longer phrase. For example 'You need the money' and 'You're a lazy idiot' becomes 'You need the money you lazy idiot'.

- Try to swap the group members between roles. By this stage of the workshop one person may be repeatedly playing Jo. Ideally s/he should be replaced so that a multiple Jo is developed. This needs to be negotiated with the group.

- Moments where Jo has already made a decision to act or do something, should be avoided. The scenes themselves will not

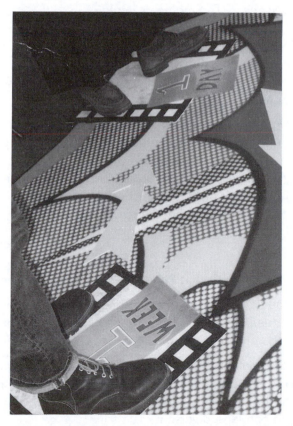

Figure 7 Blagg! from an angle. 'What happened a week/a day before the crime? Photo: The TIPP Centre

propel Jo to the offence. For example, Jo going around to a friend's house to tell her that he is going to go and buy some drugs, would not work. The decision is already made. You can avoid this problem by using the question mark sheet, and role playing the scene before Jo goes to the house. What s/he said to him/herself and how s/he made the decision in the first place would be useful because you could find a key line from it.

Trouble shooting

- *Generalities*…Participants can suggest broad ideas for why Jo committed the crime – 'He had a bad childhood', 'She was depressed' etc. Try always to push these into specifics. You want to find out an example of an incident in her/his life that made her/him like that.

- *Sitting down*…Having to stand on a square for long periods of time can be inappropriate. If someone needs to be seated, the square can be at his or her feet by the chair.

- *Similar scenes*…The moments leading up to the event are all with one character. Once you have done a scene with one person in Jo's life, suggest that the others should be with different people or situations. This is particularly the case if a male Jo, becomes surrounded by scenes with one woman identified as the source of all his problems.

- *Knowing when to stop*…This series of scenes can get over-elaborate. As it gets further into the workshop participants tend to be more confident about acting. Without cramping anybody's enthusiasm make sure they do not become over-complex and that they stick to their purpose, which is to demonstrate an incident that lead to Jo committing the offence.

★ EXERCISE 2: PUSH/SHOUT JO

1   Recap the key lines of all participants left on the sheets of paper.

2   Place the time cards at the feet of each character so that it is clear which order the scenes go in. Make this a collaborative process, asking the group as much as possible, which card goes where.

3   Place a volunteer Jo at the sheet furthest in time from the offence. Explain to the group that each person will gently push Jo from one sheet to the next whilst repeatedly saying their key line. They are seeing a condensed version of Jo's life.

4   Start this off. Usually the first time is a bit lame. Repeat it a number
     of times, taking Jo immediately back to the beginning after each
     tour, encouraging the group to shout their line and add energy to
     the exercise.

5   'Jo' will be left dazed in the middle. Ask him/her what s/he is feeling
     and thinking. It should of course be very similar to what the group
     wrote up as the original set of thoughts in Part 1.

Notes

- You can describe this exercise as a visual representation of Jo's life
  – as if you were fast-forwarding a video.

- Change the Jo actor around to avoid over-association with one
  person.

- This exercise needs energy if it is to work. It can almost be whipped
  up until it is very loud and quite forceful. It provides the impetus for
  the next exercise.

Trouble shooting

- *Over-exuberance*…The pushes should not be too strong, but there
  is an element of vocal and physical force in this exercise. This
  should be watched carefully if the group are particularly prone to
  being very physical with each other.

- *Quietness*…Some participants find it hard to speak up or repeat the
  phrase. Offer a lot of encouragement. Almost conduct this exercise,
  bringing people in, using your hands to increase volume and
  tempo.

2 The escape

WHAT?

Jo has been pushed and shouted into the middle of the explosion or ripple
effect – back to the moment of the offence which started the whole workshop
off. S/he now has an opportunity to work backwards – to escape. S/he must
now attempt to revisit each of the scenes and replay them in such a way that
s/he does not return to the offence. They must be dealt with differently to
avoid the 'push' to the centre. The group collectively find strategies to help Jo
in this task.

WHY?

It is fundamental for the Blagg! workshop to start the process of finding
alternative ways of behaving in particular situations. When finding possibilities

for Jo, some of the lessons can be transposed onto the participants' lives. Since Jo is someone similar to the group, the reasons for offending scenarios should be relevant to the lives of the whole group. The problems are not however 'solved' – a variety of alternatives might be suggested and debated. The options discovered in Blagg! are not the ideal offered by facilitators, but hopefully realistic opportunities outlined and rehearsed by the group.

Each scenario that is replayed offers an opportunity for groups to develop and improve their negotiation, communication and decision-making skills. At this stage of Blagg!, the story line of Jo is slightly sidelined and the workshop starts to blur the distinction between issues and problems in Jo's life and those in the lives of the group. Negotiating with your partner, communicating with your parents, resolving conflicts and countering peer pressure, all arise in this section and are relevant to the group in general rather than Jo specifically. Blagg! aims to conclude that alternatives can be found so that certain offences (such as the one from Part 1) do not take place.

HOW?

★ **EXERCISE 1: THE ESCAPE**

1   Ask for a volunteer to play Jo.

2   Explain that s/he is now going to redo each scene in turn starting with the nearest in time, exactly as they were done before. The group, however, has to stop each scene before it is too late and Jo is pushed towards the offence. They do this by shouting 'stop!', and replacing Jo and showing what they would do instead. A number of group members might have ideas of what could be done and all should be encouraged to demonstrate their ideas. As much as possible, this should be done in the scene rather than through discussion. Saying what you would do is one thing, having to try it in a role play is another. It is a better test of an idea.

3   Explain that once the group has helped Jo escape in every scene, the Blagg! session comes to a end.

4   A scene is successfully revisited when there is group consensus that some positive ideas have been presented. They may not be conclusive or perfect, but the group should agree that they offer improved prospects for Jo not ending up at the moment of the offence.

5   When doing a question mark sheet, the monologue should be heard again, but this time with group members stopping it to come in and argue an alternative way for Jo to view the situation. The scene will be two Jos arguing against each other.

6   The Blagg! workshop ends after the investigation of the scene furthest away in time. At this stage the facilitator should summarise the different interventions that were made and ask the group for feedback on which ones they thought were the most successful or appropriate.

Notes

- It can be valuable to make a visible note on flip chart paper of each intervention the group approved of. These can provide a useful reference for final discussions and future groupwork purposes.

Trouble shooting

- *Magic*…The basics of each scene have to remain the same. Actors cannot suddenly invent things that unfairly help them through the action. For example if Jo is drunk s/he cannot magically sober up, if Jo has no money, a £50 note cannot be found on the pavement.

- *Playing the game*…not the scene. Sometimes a participant will simply get through the scene rather than actively try to find a solution. For example in an incident where Jo is being offered drugs for the first time, on one occasion someone said, 'Do I want drugs – No. Right done that scene, which one now?' Test this response against reality. Could s/he really have done that? What stops people saying that? And ultimately 'what stopped you doing that?'

- *Giving in*…Jo says one thing and then the person they are acting with agrees and does not press their side of the argument. The other actor should be encouraged to make it as hard as possible for Jo. They can also be substituted if the group thinks an alternative approach is needed. If the person playing against Jo makes it tougher, this will also make it more difficult for the 'playing the game' response mentioned above. It is important to note, however, that normally you cannot replace other people. In real life we do not have the power to make those around us suddenly or magically behave differently.

- *No alternative*…The group insists that in a particular scene Jo has no alternative but to commit the crime. First, do not take this at face value. Push it, as often a new strategy will emerge. If the group are insistent you can either insist that Jo does find an alternative 'because of what happens to him/her afterwards', or accept that in some circumstances it is too late and Jo will be too committed to making the incident happen. It is clear, however, that there must be a situation when it would not have been too late. This should be directed into a discussion about at what point they can still avoid the offence. The question mark sheet can be used to find a moment before the one from where the offence was inevitable.

- *The unchangeable*…There are things that cannot be re-negotiated however 'pro-socially' you act. If Jo's father died at an early age this cannot be changed – it is a given fact. The pain and hurt situations such as this might have caused, should be recognised and discussed. However, it is always Jo's decisions and actions in response to these 'given facts' which are crucial for the purpose of the workshop. It is possible and important to develop a debate about these 'givens' when they do arise.

3 Deroling

Whilst it is valuable to end Blagg! with a final discussion and feedback session, it can also be important to supplement this with a deroling exercise. If the session has been particularly intense this is strongly advised.

WHAT?

In the first exercise an empty chair is interviewed as Jo Blaggs, providing the group with the opportunity to give a piece of advice or make one final comment. The other two exercises are winding down games.

WHY?

If some members of the group have over-identified with Jo, they can internalise his/her problems. The chair exercise recreates Jo as someone clearly different from the group, and ensures that the boundaries of what is real and what is fiction are re-established. The winding down games enable a group to leave on a positive note. They bring the group together in an activity that mediates the serious focus on the offending behaviour work.

HOW?

★ EXERCISE 1: THE CHAIR

1   Place an empty chair in front of the group.

2   Tell the group that this chair is now occupied by Jo (an invisible one!).

3   Ask each person in turn to either offer Jo one piece of advice, or make one final comment.

4   There is little need to comment further yourself on the group's words.

5   A variation of this exercise can be done without the chair, with each person saying what they think are the similarities and the differences between them and Jo.

Notes

- Make sure you and the other staff give the advice and make a comment as well. This will obviously contribute to the exercise.

★ **EXERCISE 2: THE CLAP**

1   Stand the group in a circle.

2   Ask people to hold their hands out in front of themselves, a short way apart as though they were about to clap.

3   Instruct the group that they are all going to clap at exactly the same time without one person being the leader.

4   After a signal and silence, stand and wait for the clap.

5   Repeat the exercise until the clap is close to perfect.

Notes

- Silence is important as it helps concentration and adds to the exercise's tension.
- Do not let the exercise fail! Offer congratulations if they are close.
- If appropriate, you can add in the instructions that as soon as it is done, the workshop is over and everyone can leave. This creates a tidy ending to the workshop.

Trouble shooting

- *Cheating*…One person sneakily tries to lead the clap. Do not worry too much. Impressing on the group that what they are trying to do is hard and requires skill, can often diffuse the desire to disrupt.

★ **EXERCISE 3: ONE TO TEN**

1   Stand the group in a circle.

2   Tell them that they will now count to ten, one person at a time, with no person leading and without the numbers going around in any order. If two people say a number at the same time you have to start again.

3   Keep starting again until you get all the way.

Notes

- It is often quite hard to explain this exercise. Start to run it rather than rely on an over-elaborate description that can confuse. Once it gets going everyone will pick it up.
- It can help the exercise if everyone closes his or her eyes.
- The same point as above. You can add in the instruction that as soon as it is done, the workshop is over and everyone can leave.

Trouble shooting

- *Never reaching ten…set the number lower!*

FURTHER DEVELOPMENT

The work of Blagg! can be integrated fully into wider offending behaviour, social skills and conflict resolution courses. The following are some suggestions on how to do this. This is a selection of ideas and is in no way conclusive.

1 Following on

(a) *Jo's future.* What does the group think (i) *should* happen to Jo and (ii) *would* happen to Jo? The difference between responses (i) and (ii) can be discussed. This can be done in opposing debating teams or a role play court case acted out. A court scene can be a good opportunity for a detailed examination of the whole incident. Video recording can be useful here.

(b) *Jo's punishment.* The group may have decided what would happen to Jo in the court scene. Now they can be given the opportunity to say 'what would work with Jo?/what would stop her/him offending?' This will often lead to a discussion of why people stop etc., which can be useful. To make it more animated, mock interviews can be set up – Jo with a fictional probation officer, Jo with girlfriend/boyfriend or family, Jo with prison education officer etc. See how Jo reacts with different pressures on him/her to change.

(c) *The long term.* In groups or individually, a brief life sketch has to be created for Jo. What is s/he doing at thirty, forty, fifty etc.? Different sketches can be compared and contrasted. Group members will paint rosy pictures and some very depressing ones. The reasons for these different perspectives can be investigated. This result can be reproduced deliberately by asking clients to come up with the best possible and the worst possible lives for Jo (ensuring they base their predictions on the existing information). Role play interviews of clients playing an older Jo can further analyse how s/he arrived at that point.

(d) *Blagg!* examines several incidents that lead up to the crime but by no means all of them. The group should be encouraged to outline other moments in Jo's life which lead to crime or conflict. These can be talked through, acted out, videoed, written about etc. A more detailed life history can be created.

(e) *Interventions and alternative action.* During Blagg! the group tries to intervene in incidents to prevent Jo arriving back at the crime. The methods of intervention can be practised over and over again. The other 'moments' outlined under (d) should also be looked at. What else could Jo have done in these situations? Talk through/act out the alternatives. How realistic are they?

(f) *The group* can be asked to find similar moments in their own lives. When does the problem Jo faced in that situation occur in your life? These could be role played and interventions sought as in Blagg! itself.

2 Repeat Blagg!

This is stating the obvious, but Blagg! does change each time it is played and it can be replayed with the same group looking at different offences. This can often enforce what has been learnt in the first playing.

3 Blagg! with a real 'Jo'

The structure of the workshop can be used to examine the real behaviour of one member of the group. The effect on their victims, how they got into offending and how they could avoid it in the future could all be tackled directly. It is important, however, that when focusing on one individual, the other members of the group are not left out.

   The real Jo exercises can either follow the practical exercises of the Blagg! workshop, or the workshop can be used as a structure for discussion. Concentrating on one person should only be done if the context of the work allows it and there are appropriate support mechanisms in place.

4 Beliefs

In getting groups to look at the effects of crime on their victims, Blagg! is starting the process of challenging individuals about their beliefs and values. A whole session could be handed over just to this, expanding on the workshop and developing individuals' awareness of other perspectives. Interviews with victims can be role played, television-style chat shows can be recreated on pertinent issues, and the effects on family members fully examined.

5 Social skills

Blagg! deals a lot with communication and other social skills. The techniques and metaphors of Blagg! can be re-used to develop the work further. For example, family interactions, arguments and peer pressure resistance can all be examined using the 'stop rules'. Role plays can include real people or previously created 'fictional' characters.

6 Decisions and consequences

Working to increase people's consequential thinking is an important part of offending behaviour work. Blagg! again opens up this process but certainly does not conclude it. The exploration in Blagg! of decisions taken by one character in several key moments, needs to be expanded into the decisions that group members make in a wide variety of situations. In all cases, these must be linked to potential consequences – for the offenders, their family and the victims.

As before, the Blagg! structure can both be the focus of discussion or the practical exercises can be used to look at consequences in more detail. Tableaux of incidents can be put next to tableaux of consequences. 'Cartooning' of offences can be done in three dimensions rather than on paper with a tableau for each moment of the incident. Photography can be a good way to record this. The techniques should be adapted to link *situation – thinking – decision – consequence*, and compare *same situation – different thinking – different decision – what kind of consequence?*

Connected to decision making is a type of risk assessment – how risky is it to get involved with this or that activity? Once the risk is fully assessed, a more informed decision can be made. Charting the risks in each situation that Jo was in, or the group have been in, can be a useful exercise. Challenging a group to see all the risks involved, and pushing them to consider not just the most immediate, is an important part of the work. Risks are not only about getting caught, but the impact of your actions on your family and on others.

7 Alternative Blagg!

Staff have already used Blagg! in many different ways. For example the Jo Blaggs character has been created as the victim of a particular offence rather than the perpetrator (Hughes 1998). The whole workshop then focused, using the same exercises, on the victim's perspective. Similarly the central incident could change radically. If it were a divorce, the workshop would be very different, if it were an important decision in your life such as leaving home, again the workshop would be shifted dramatically. Whilst all the exercises would not necessarily follow easily if these changes were made, it is important to point out that the structure is there to be creatively reinterpreted.

8 Video

Blagg! and further exercises in effect create a life story. This can be made very simply into a film by videoing each scene in an order decided by the group. Different endings can be put on, showing the variety of possible directions in Jo's life.

THE END?

I hope that this manual provides a comprehensive guide to the Blagg! workshop. Please use it as you see fit and how it best suits your objectives. Whether you follow it religiously, browse or dip; the primary aim is that it helps the worker make effective use of the Blagg! workshop.

Pump! – The History

The development of the Pump! programme was, for the TIPP Centre, an obvious move forward from the Blagg! workshop. With Blagg!, Greater Manchester Probation Service (GMPS) had asked the organisation to create a single workshop for incorporation into wider programmes. In 1994, partly after the success of Blagg!, GMPS extended this by commissioning the Centre to create a whole programme. The broad commission which triggered the research into Blagg! was replaced by a very specific brief. They asked for a full anger management course that could become a core programme across the service.

The development of the programme, however, followed a similar pattern to the creation of Blagg! A team of probation staff, all of whom had had experience in delivering programmes for violent offenders, were brought together as a liaison committee to co-operate with staff from the TIPP Centre.[1] Between February and July 1994, a series of meetings took place with presentations from TIPP followed by detailed feedback from the probation officers. Whilst this process has been described in detail elsewhere (Thompson 1996), it is worth covering several of the important moments here.

First there were some key assumptions or beliefs held at the outset and taken into this process which need to be acknowledged. For example, amongst all the staff there was an agreement that anger in itself is not a negative emotion. Anger it was agreed can be a force for good. Righteous anger has been the inspiration behind many positive and progressive individuals and social movements, and the programme was, therefore, not simply going to be an attempt to nullify the emotion in itself. Whilst 'anger management' is one of those phrases that obscures as much as it reveals, it was important to emphasise that the course would be developing skills in the management of an emotion, not the suppression of one. This touches upon a second assumption which was the importance of dealing at the level of skill development, and although

[1] Other than myself, the team included Jocelyn Meall, the designer and Michael Balfour, the Programme Development Worker at the TIPP Centre at that time.

explosive anger might have some deep-seated causes, these could not be the central focus of the programme. A short course could only hope to be valuable when working with participants on practical techniques for the future. Resolving underlying pain and abuse would be a much longer and harder process and, ideally, should go hand in hand with a course such as the one we were seeking to create.

The second aspect of this process worth noting is that the research into the course was inspired by the practice existing in probation settings and in particular in the work of the US psychologist, Novaco. GMPS had an intuitive belief that to deal with clients' anger, a course should perhaps use role play and active, participatory techniques. They commissioned TIPP with an understanding that an issue as dynamic as violence could not rely solely on paper and pen exercises. Whilst it is a truism to state that theatre is based in many instances on situations of conflict, the assumption was made that this should be reversed, with situations of conflict learning from theatre. The clinical trials pioneered by Novaco during the 1970s echoed this understanding and provided for us the theoretical bridge between research into anger control and theatre practice (Novaco 1975). Novaco based his anger control programmes on a series of training exercises for his subjects.

These included: '"thought stopping", where individuals were encouraged to counter the internal thought processes that provoked their anger, and "stress inoculation", where participants were exposed to simulated situations and taught strategies to maintain calm' (Thompson 1996, p.71).

The key point here was that all the techniques required 'simulation' so that skills could be developed in laboratory conditions. The development team's research into the work of anger control specialists such as Novaco clearly demonstrated that quasi-theatrical approaches were central. His work echoed our desire to create a workshop space where behaviours could be discovered and rehearsed. Simulation was exactly what we would be doing in creating role plays and improvisations. Our workshop was in some ways to mimic the anger control researcher's laboratory. Novaco's ideas were thus incorporated into the programme from the outset, not only because he was internationally recognised as a leader in the field of anger control, but also because of this immediate link to theatrical processes.

The third moment of programme development to discuss, initially came as a warning. Very early on in the devising process, one probation officer from the staff team related an anecdote about a previous anger management programme she had been involved in running. Several months after the end of the course, one of her clients met and spoke with her. He was pleased about the impact of the course on his life and claimed that he could now control his anger.

However, he went on to say that he could also now control people around him
– 'rather than hitting her, all I need to do is sit there quietly and she does
exactly as I want' (Thompson 1996, p.71). One type of behaviour had been
replaced by another, but the consequence for the victim was much the same.
This made us all stop and think very hard. For a start, it emphasised the need to
split anger management from domestic violence programmes. Whilst there are
techniques which cross over between the two, domestic abusers do not
necessarily get angry when they abuse they partners. In addition, there are a
complex array of power and attitudinal issues which need addressing. Many
probation services now accept this logic and run separate programmes for men
convicted of violence against their partners and those convicted of other
violence. This said, we felt that the programme we were to develop, whilst it
was geared at the general violent offender category, had to take into account
these other types of controlling behaviours. Whilst men on the course might
have index offences related to anger outbursts in bars for example, they may
also have substantial but perhaps hidden domestic violence histories. Two
words thus became key in all the initial development period – power and
control. Loosing self-control in an angry outburst is a means of maintaining or
exerting power over another person. However, in maintaining self-control, as
in the anecdote above, a person can still exert abusive power over another. The
relation between control of self and control of others was vital and it was
important not to concentrate only on the control of self. Power and control
thus became intersecting and vital ideas to weave through the programme.

The fourth key point from the development stage to note is the tendency of
the creative planning process to overcomplicate workshop structures, and lose
itself in technical detail. This was exactly what happened during the
development of Blagg!, and it happened again with Pump! At one stage in
designing Pump! we had developed unfathomable graphs on the floor which
plotted the relationship at certain moments between our key ideas of power
and control. What I called in Marian Liebmann's book *Arts Approaches to
Conflict* 'a mathematical approach to conflict' (Thompson 1996, p.76). It owed
more to the complex statistical analysis chapters of Novaco (1975) than the
work of theatre practitioners. We soon realised that we had to rediscover our
sense of theatre, simplify the narrative structure and translate graphs into
useable, accessible metaphors. This we did (eventually), but it is significant that
during both Blagg! and Pump! a similar refocusing was needed. It is as if on
entering the territory of a different discipline, with the simultaneous need to
embrace an unfamiliar language in order to communicate with new partners,
existing knowledge is forgotten. Only once a level of fluency is achieved in that
new language, is our own language and practice returned to and refigured. This

re-figuring, rather than leading to a dilution of two approaches can lead to a hybridisation which creates a stronger and more dynamic practice. This process, to me, is now a predictable and desirable part of the process of multidisciplinary work. While devising the Pump! programme it was a tough moment to negotiate, but it should in fact be welcomed as a necessary part of an arts dialogue with a non-arts based agency.

The final point to be made about this process is linked to the notion of language. While the TIPP team were researching anger management theories and the probation team were developing an understanding of approaches to participatory theatre, it became clear that notions of the vocabulary of violence were crucial. Narratives of violence are full of signals and codes that become understood in different ways by different groups. When one young offender says 'I gave him a good talking to', this is often a rhetorical device to hint at violence. Members of groups will often make a comment and add a knowing wink or nod, as if to say 'you know what I mean'. These rhetorics become methods to distance, excuse, minimise or simply to self-censor descriptions of behaviour. Rather than slipping into this rhetoric, we felt the course needed to shape its own. We wanted to create verbal markers that could be defined by the course programme and owned by the participants. We aimed, therefore, from the outset to develop a language which, whilst still a rhetoric in itself, was the new rhetoric for the course. Members we hoped would use and take control of it. To counter the mystification of much client language, the course was to develop its own simple and accessible code.[2]

Gradually over this period an eight-session course evolved, split into three sections called the Pump!, Jack! and the Box. Soon the name of the whole course was shortened to Pump! The programme was piloted in two probation areas and a detailed evaluation done by GMPS. The comments from this were incorporated into the course as it appears here. During these initial pilots all clients filled in pre- and post-questionnaires and these were analysed to assess changes in attitudes to anger and notions of self-control. The following comes from an early version of this evaluation:

> It is clear that from the clients' responses that by the end of each session they had mostly grasped the skill being taught and were able to relate to how that skill could be used in person problem-solving. Clients were introduced to a new vocabulary and became able to apply the vocabulary to their own situation.... Staff felt that the project had been successful and

2   See sessions 1 to 3 in the manual.

that clear commitment had been demonstrated by the group members. (Practice Development Unit, 1995, quoted in Thompson 1996, p.90)

Since these pilots, the workshop has been run in a number of prisons, probation areas and with young offenders with anger problems. The programme is now the core anger management programme for GMPS run centrally by the Probation Practice Team staff. Any client in the Greater Manchester region receiving a court order to attend an anger management course will go on this programme. In addition there are two prisons that have staff trained to use it as a core programme.

The manual within this edition was developed after the programme had been run for some time. This was important in that a course can only become stable after it has been tried and tested in several different locations and with a variety of course participants. Although here it is fixed as eight sessions, already various groups have adapted it to fit the requirements of their institution or agency. One organisation has extended it slightly and another has had to condense it because of regime restrictions. Whilst I would encourage a flexible approach, it is important that the key learning objectives of the different stages of the programme are not lost. Since 1994 the programme has been run in community settings and in secure environments. It has been run with adult probationers with relatively minor convictions for violence, with sex offenders in a therapeutic wing of a prison and with patients in secure units with mental health diagnoses. Each group will approach the course in a different way. Professionals – whether they are from the probation, prison or health care services – must examine the programme to be sure that it is appropriate for their groups. A clear approach to referral, back-up and support for clients before, during and after a programme must be in place. In order to devise the Pump! programme, a strong dialogue between different professionals needed to be created and sustained. A similar open negotiation between the course, the staff who are to implement it and the setting in which it is to be run, is vital if its benefits are to be realised.

Good luck and welcome to Pump!

The Pump! Manual

INTRODUCTION

Welcome to the Pump! manual. The following represents a detailed guide for staff using the programme. Obviously in running Pump!, staff members' own pace and style will be incorporated into the course. This is to be encouraged if the programme is to successfully become part of, rather than an addition to other work. However, as much as possible, the programme should remain whole with the underlying session objectives being maintained.

Staff are encouraged to use this manual for internal training first, before techniques are used with client groups. For programme integrity reasons individual sessions should not be run outside the whole course structure, unless they are to be incorporated into other structured groupwork programmes. However, individual exercises in this manual may be used separately to complement other groupwork.

TYPE AND SIZE OF GROUP

The Pump! programme has been run with court-ordered probation clients with violence convictions or acknowledged anger management problems. It has been run in prisons with general location prisoners (volunteers) and it has also been used on specialist wings/wards for particularly violent inmates/patients. Although it has been run with clients with mental health diagnoses, staff should take extra precaution when using this programme with clients suffering from various types of psychosis. This is not to say that they would never be appropriate for such a programme. The programme could be run with younger age groups and some school age people. Staff working with these age groups should be careful to ensure the language and exercises described here are adapted for their groups.

Whilst the programme was not only designed for men, to date it has only been run with men's groups. Careful consideration needs to be given before having mixed groups. I would not rule it out altogether, but only rare circumstances would make it appropriate. Perhaps mixed groups in schools would be one of these occasions. An all women's group would be appropriate, although staff should take extra care in adapting the course to fit their needs. Particular attention should be paid to the specific ways in which some vulnerable women internalise their anger and how this can be manifested in self-harm.

The programme can be run with as few as three and up to ten participants. The greater the number, the harder it is to focus on one individual's particular problems. The smaller the number, the more intense the experience can be for the participants.

It is important to have at least two facilitators, one of whom is from the agency/institution where the group is taking place. This is so that any issues arising from the group can be fed back properly into the work of the organisation.

SPACE

You will need a moderately sized groupwork room free of tables (if possible) with a chair for each participant. In addition, you will need a flip chart pad and pens or another method for recording information. Finally, insulation or masking tape is needed for the floor in session six.

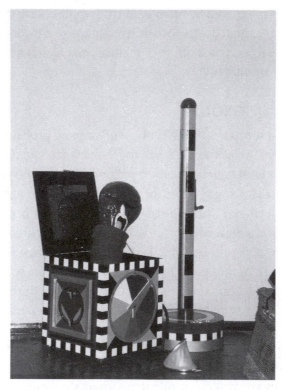

Figure 8 The Pump! Photo: The TIPP Centre

As with Blagg!, the Pump! course was originally designed with a set. This included a large outsized grotesque jack-in-the-box, and a huge three dimensional anger thermometer. This manual is written for use without these. For further information on the props please contact the TIPP Centre.

TIMINGS

The course is split into eight two-hour sessions. How these are spread over time depends of course on the agency/institution running the course. I suggest, however, that there is some gap between sessions and they do not all happen over four days. An optimum would be two sessions per week over four weeks.

It is important to note that just running these eight sessions should not be seen as the end of 'anger management'. A course such as this starts a process, or comes in the middle of an ongoing process. It is vital that the course sits within a wider plan for the needs of each individual participant.

DESCRIBING PUMP!

All participants on an anger management course need to be selected beforehand by the agency/institution. A pre-group interview should assess whether a person is suitable for groupwork, and also explain to the potential participant the style of the group. Pump! can be described as participatory groupwork involving drama and/or role play. It is important to emphasise that rather than just talking about situations, the group will be exploring them on their feet.

Each institution will have its own procedures for referral and clearly these should be followed carefully. It should be noted that participants who are very nervous, are in complete denial or who are outwardly aggressive/hostile will very likely be unsuitable for Pump! The programme has proved particularly positive with individuals who recognise they have an anger problem, but currently do not know what to do about it.

THE COURSE AIMS AND OBJECTIVES

Course aim: for participants to identify, examine and learn strategies to manage their anger/involvement in violent situations.

Course objectives: at the end of the course participants will have:

1   Learnt the differences between Knocks, Wind-ups and Pumps and how these contribute to anger situations.

2   Practised strategies for dealing with these components of anger situations.

3   Examined violent incidents and the thoughts, feelings and triggers behind them in their and other group members' lives.

4   Practised strategies for dealing with these moments and examined the beliefs and attitudes behind them.

5   Examined the links between violence and other controlling behaviours.

6   Practised dealing with anger and conflict situations assertively.

7   Reviewed the course and set targets for the future.

Figure 9 Michael Balfour running a Pump! group. Photo: The TIPP Centre.

THE SESSIONS
1 The Pump!

Session aim: to introduce the group to Knocks, Wind-ups and Pumps and examine situations in which they occur.

Session objectives: at the end of the session participants will have:

1   Been introduced to the course aims and objectives.

2   Had the ground rules explained.

3   Been introduced to the participatory style of the group

4   Been introduced to the idea of an 'anger thermometer' and had the terms Knock, Wind-up and Pump practically explained.

5   Examined anger scenarios and used the language of Knocks, Wind-ups and Pumps to analyse them.

THE SESSION
(a) Introduction to the course
The whole course aims and objectives are briefly explained. Any questions on these and the practical arrangements for the course are to be answered.

(b) Ground rules
These should be set according to the established groupwork rules of the agency/establishment/institution where the course is being run. The group should be involved in this process and contribute to agreed rules. The responsibility to actively participate in the course should be included here.

(c) Introduce the aims and objectives for this session
These should be read through and any questions taken. Explain that any terms used will become clear during the session.

(d) Warming up the group
Explain that this group is 'participatory' and is about demonstrating, or showing what people mean, not just talking through incidents. The course will ask people to participate in role plays and active 'on their feet' exercises.

The warm-ups are to develop the group's focus, relax them and introduce them to each other. They are both mental and physical, preparing people to engage both physically and mentally with the course.

MENTAL WARM-UPS
Introduce your partner
Ask each group member to turn to the person next to him or her. They have to find out three pieces of information. The person's name and two facts about them. Give them a very short time to complete this. Once all appear to be ready, ask each person to report back to the whole group, introducing their partner and the two facts.

PM/President for the day
Ask the group to imagine they are each the Prime Minister/President for the day. Around the circle, each person has to say what he or she would do to make

the world a better place for everybody. Allow a discussion to develop about different group member's choices.

PHYSICAL WARM-UPS

Stand up if…

Going around the group each person asks a question of the group. Participants must stand up if their reply is positive, and stay seated if it is negative.

Examples:

- Has anyone had a cup of tea this morning?
- Did anyone not want to come this morning?

The questions should start quite gently but they can become more probing. Whilst all members should ask a question – the facilitators could decide to ask more to find out information from the group. Try and make this exercise move fast so people are getting up and down rapidly.

Anyone who…?

As per 'Fruit Bowl' in the Blagg! manual, but the person in the middle asks 'anyone who…is wearing black, has an earring, etc'. If your response to the question is positive you get up and change chairs. Facilitators should try and ask questions to get as many people up as possible.

This exercise should follow on rapidly from the one above. Alternatively it can be used instead of 'Stand up if…'.

(e) Introducing 'participation'

It is important to demonstrate what the course means by 'participation'. Of course it is best to do this actively – rather than verbally.

WHAT'S THE STORY?

This exercise is a repeat of the same exercise in the Blagg! manual. It is a crucial starting point to each course. It is rewritten here (in the style of this manual) to save readers from referring back when using the manual.

Take two volunteers – make it easy to volunteer by saying that they do not have to do anything! One is asked to stand at the back of the room away from the group, the other towards the front, near the group. They should be on a diagonal and not directly behind one another. They should stand neutrally with their hands by their sides.

The facilitator asks the group – 'What's the story?' What does this represent? Any reply is accepted and repeated so all the group hear it. Keep asking until all replies are exhausted.

Repeat this exercise, but this time ask the person standing furthest away to take one step forward. What differences do people notice? How does this change the story? Keep repeating this until the person at the back has moved past the one in front.

Having completed the whole sequence, ask the group for the most popular suggestion from any of the moments – or images. Return to that image and ask if the suggestion were true, what would each person be about to say. Find a single line of dialogue for each person standing. Check that each 'volunteer' has understood their line, and then ask them (on the count of three) to start the scene. Once the two lines are said the audience should be encouraged to burst into 'spontaneous' applause.

This final section can be done after analysing only one position or image if the group has less time.

PROCESSING

It is important to make it clear to the group why this exercise has been run and also take their feedback. 'What's the story?' gets people on their feet and it generates a small role play in a non-pressurised and safe way. Most importantly, however, it encourages participants to look really hard at what is in front of them. You are forcing your group to 'look twice' and not accept their first reading.

Ask the group what they felt the significance of this exercise was, for a course on anger management. It needs to be made clear that there were no right answers in individual's analysis of the images. Ask the group how the idea of 'various readings' might be translated into the real world.

PAIRED IMAGES

The first part of this exercise is a repeat of the same exercise in the Blagg! manual. Like 'What's the story?' it is a crucial starting point to each course. It is rewritten here (in the style of this manual) to save readers from referring back when using the manual.

Ask the group to get into pairs. One is to be the modeller, the other is to be modelled. You can use a phrase such as sculptor and clay if it helps clarify the roles. Demonstrate with one volunteer, or your co-worker, how each person is going to model their partner. You can put a person in a position you like by moving them directly and gently. When it comes to difficult parts such as the face, demonstrating for the 'clay' to copy is allowed. The person modelling should avoid using words or simply doing a whole action for the person to copy.

Ask the group to create images of particular characters — a father, a footballer, the police etc.

When they are confident with these, ask them to create images of emotions — anger, fear, happiness etc.

Swap between modeller and modelled after each new image. Every image created should be analysed (the degree depends on time). In particular, the similarities and the differences between the group's images should be examined. As in the previous exercise, open questions should be asked when analysing the images — multiple interpretations should be encouraged. 'What do they see?', 'what images do they like?', 'what do they mean to them?' etc.

Take one person in an image and place your fist above their head. Explain that this is the sign for a thought bubble. Explain that when you use this during the course you are asking for a person's thoughts. Ask the group what they think this person is thinking. Repeat and accept all their contributions. Open your palm above the head. Explain that this is the sign for speech. Ask the group what they think this person is saying (or is about to say). Again repeat and accept all their contributions. Put you fist on your heart. Explain that this is the sign for feeling. Finally ask the group what they think this person is feeling.

Conclude this exercise by explaining that all these techniques will be used throughout the course. In particular, there will be a major emphasis on the links between real incidents, and the thoughts and feelings that accompany them.

(f) Introduction to the Pump! course language

This session looks at three prompts that can fuel an angry or violent reaction. They are Knocks, Wind-ups and Pumps. Draw a large thermometer on a flip chart. Explain that the top of this thermometer is where an outburst or violent incident occurs. Knocks, Wind-ups and Pumps are what push the mercury upwards. Each in their own way or combined can result in the 'temper-ature' rising.

Each term will be explained using the same structure:

1   Explanation

2   Demonstration

3   Practice

4   Discussion

(g) Knocks

EXPLANATION

Knocks are given facts that cannot be changed, happen to all people and are not done maliciously. If you go out and it starts to pour with rain and you get annoyed then this is a Knock. You get a bill, the TV set blows up. These are Knocks. They are facts of life. They are not intentional acts of provocation. *You cannot blame anyone else for a Knock.*

DEMONSTRATION

Ask for two volunteers. Sculpt them into an image of a postman/woman handing a bill to a householder. Ask the group what they see. What to them is going on and where the Knock is in the scene? It does not matter if they do not pick up exactly the intended Knock – if they agree on an act which you agree is a Knock, go with it. This image is broadly related to a theme of not blaming the messenger and therefore any 'bad news' is relevant.

Place your fist above the head of the householder. Ask the group what they think the person is thinking. Put your fist on your heart and ask the group what they think the person is feeling. Ask the group whether this will have made the person move up the scale on the thermometer.

Check the group is clear why this is a Knock. You cannot blame the postman/woman – the messenger.

PRACTICE

Ask the group to turn to the person next to them to form a pair. A co-worker can opt in or out to make an even number. Each pair is to discuss what Knocks have happened to each of them recently. They must chose one and create an image/tableau of it.

Each image is shown, and the rest of the group members must say what they see. Again, whilst it is worth checking whether they have guessed right, anything they say – if it is agreed to be a Knock – is a right answer.

Use the 'fist above the head/fist on heart' to access what the person being Knocked thought and felt at the time. Ask how much this might have moved someone up the anger thermometer. If there is a person doing the Knocking, it is worth checking what group members think they were thinking as well. If the group is in disagreement about whether an act is deliberate or not, it is useful to suggest that a person Knocking another can have very innocent intentions.

DISCUSSION

Discuss the whole idea of the Knock. Ask the group to feedback other examples, or what was talked through in the pairs. Debate and disagreement is good here. If there is disagreement over whether something is a Knock or not, always refer it to the group for comment. Try as much as possible to find consensus amongst those present. A last resort is to return to the definition you have here in the Appendix.

(h) Wind-ups

EXPLANATION

A Wind-up is a deliberate act. It can be an attitude someone has, it can be a provocative action or comment, or it can be a taunt or threat. It has the intention of winding you up. A Wind-up can be combined with a Knock. It is highly likely that any response to another's Wind-up will be interpreted as a Wind-up itself. *Winding up a Wind-up is dangerous.*

DEMONSTRATION

Ask for two new volunteers (you could use the same two as before if this seems appropriate). Sculpt them into a very similar image as before, but this time the postman/woman is laughing or somehow mocking the householder as they hand over the bill.

Ask the group what they see. What to them is going on and where is the Wind-up in the scene? As before it does not matter if they do not pick up exactly the intended Wind-up – but it will be pretty clear!

Using the 'fist above the head/fist on heart' ask the group what they think the householder is thinking and feeling. How does this differ from the previous scene? Have they moved higher up the anger thermometer?

Check that the group are clear that this is a Wind-up. Discuss with the group the significance of the statement – 'Winding up a Wind-up is dangerous'.

PRACTICE

Again in pairs, ask the group to discuss what Wind-ups have happened to them recently. They should choose one and create an image/tableau. Each image is shown to the group as before, and they must say what they see. Again, whilst it is worth checking whether they have guessed right, anything they say – if it is agreed to be a Wind-up – is a right answer.

Use the 'fist above the head/fist on heart' to access the thoughts and feelings of the person being wound up. If the facilitator believes what has been shown is in fact a Knock, use the 'fist above the head' to access the thoughts of the person who is supposedly winding the other up. You, your co-worker, or a group member might suggest thoughts that clearly demonstrate that there is in fact no malice – no deliberate attempt to provoke.

Check that the group is clear as to the difference between Knocks and Wind-ups. It must be emphasised that Knocks are in fact much more common that Wind-ups (the group might take some convincing of this). Recreate tableaux that could be confusing to illustrate that often *Knocks are interpreted as Wind-ups*. If a tableau has not come up in the session you could prepare one in advance with your co-worker:

- The landlord Knocks a customer by not serving him/her because 'last orders' has been called.

- A customer Knocks your drink over.

- A friend Knocks you by not repaying a debt, etc.

By accessing the thoughts of the landlord, customer, and friend, it can be illustrated that it is dangerous to assume an incident is a Wind-up when it could be a Knock.

Another addition that can be made here is to chose one pair's image and ask the group to recreate it, but this time as if the person supposedly doing the winding up were retelling the story. Ask the group how this might change the image. It is worth reminding the group that in the 'What's the story?' exercise different interpretations were made. Similarly during this exercise, they may be creating images of their interpretations of events rather than images of reality.

DISCUSSION

Ask the group for feedback on what other Wind-ups they identified when in the pairs. Clarify whether these are Wind-ups or Knocks. The more this is debated the better. Do not expect complete consensus at this stage as the debate over these terms should continue throughout the course.

(i) Pumps – or pumping thoughts

EXPLANATION

A Pump is an internal thought that pushes you up the anger thermometer. It is a thought that pumps you up in response to an external incident – usually a Knock or a Wind-up. Pumping thoughts are the personal interpretation and justification of events that promote and stimulate your anger and sometimes violence.

DEMONSTRATION

Recreate the first tableau of the postman/woman 'knocking' the householder. Say that this scene now ends in violence. Ask the group to suggest the final image – the moment of violence. See/sculpt this and discuss it.

Now ask the group to fill in the story. Return to the original image and suggest that there are two or three more images between that moment and the image of the violence that they have already created. What are they? Get the group to move the original image into the new moments, ending with the image of violence. Create a sequence.

Watch the sequence in rapid succession. You can clap your hands from one image to the next. Each one is done while still and in silence, from the bill arriving to the postman/woman being hit (or whatever the group members have decided).

Return to image one. Use the 'fist over the head' to ask what the Pumping thoughts are in the householder's head. What does this person say to himself or herself that pushes them up the anger thermometer? Repeat this for each image, recording the key phrases. At the end, you should have a list of possible pumping thoughts for the sequence. Remember Pumping thoughts are those that stimulate anger – they are not just reflective thoughts. Examples might be:

- 'How dare s/he look at me like that!'
- 'Who does s/he think s/he is!'
- 'I am always getting treated like this.'
- 'S/he deserves a kicking!'

PRACTICE

Returning to their pairs, the group should now complete this exercise on either their Knock images or their Wind-up images. It is worth directing some of the group to do Knocks leading to violence. This would illustrate that Pumps are often the misinterpretation of an event. This is valuable because there is a tendency to believe that violence is a legitimate response to a Wind-up.

If the pairs are unlikely to work comfortably on their own, each pair could be worked on in front of the whole group, with Pumping thoughts being accessed publicly by the facilitator. Time constraints might not allow for every pair to be used. If this is the case, take one or two that demonstrate very different incidents.

Each pair should end up with a short list of Pumping thoughts.

DISCUSSION

Discuss the phrases that have been recorded, checking that the group is clear when a thought is and is not a real Pump. The key point to emphasise is that it is the interpretation of an incident that leads to violence, not the event itself.

(j) Spot the Knock!

PART 1

Divide the group into two teams. Each team must create a series of tableaux/images that demonstrate two Knocks and two Wind-ups – a short story. Whilst it is preferable for these to be still moments, a group can move in 'mime' between them if they feel it would be easier. These are then shown with the observing group having to note down the Knocks and Wind-ups that they see. Check the results to see if each group has guessed the right Knocks and not missed any. What often happens here is that the observers note many more Knocks and Wind-ups than the group presenting intended. This is worth discussion in itself.

PART 2

Each team must repeat their images/scene. This time the observing group must stop the action when they choose (by shouting 'freeze!' or 'stop!') and add the Pumping thoughts. What was this character thinking, what thoughts might pump them up the anger thermometer? Of course the facilitator or co-worker can stop the scene as well.

PART 3

If there is time in this session, ask for a final repeat, but this time each group observing adds pressure by stopping the action and suggesting further Knocks or Wind-ups. The characters must deal with these, and the observers must suggest how far up the thermometer the character has moved. It is difficult not to have movement in this section, so this should be allowed.

Ask the group for a short feedback as to how the main characters in both the scenes could have moved through them without resorting to violence. At what point was it too late?

(k) Concluding the session

Check with the group that they have understood the key terms – Knock, Wind-up and Pump. Explain that in the following session they will be examining strategies for dealing with them.

If the course is using any form of anger diary, hand it out at this stage and ask the group to fill in at least one incident for the following week. This should be broken down into:

- Description of incident.
- Whether it was a Knock, a Wind-up or a combination of the two.
- What were the Pumping thoughts?

- Any other thoughts.
- What were the feelings?

See Appendix 1 for a model diary hand-out.

2 Deflating the Pump!

Session aim: to introduce the group to the strategies for dealing with Knocks, Wind-ups and Pumps.

Session objectives: at the end of the session participants will have:

1   Discussed the physiological signs of anger.

2   Suggested and practised strategies for dealing with Knocks and Wind-ups.

3   Examined and practised thought-stopping and self-calming statements.

THE SESSION

(a) *Recap of last week*

Very briefly go over the terms introduced in the previous session to check the group has fully understood them.

(b) *Introduce the aims and objectives of the session*

(c) *Anger diaries*
MENTAL WARM-UP

Ask each member of the group for one good thing that has happened to them that week and one bad thing.

Use this as a way into the anger diaries. Ask for feedback from these or feedback on one of the 'bad things' announced in the previous exercise. If anyone is prepared to talk about an incident from the week in detail this should be encouraged. This should provide an opportunity for the individual to get it off their chest (an anger management technique in itself), but also for the group to use the Knock, Wind-up and Pump language to discuss a real incident.

PHYSICAL WARM-UP
Knots

Ask the group to stand in a circle. They then should place one arm into the centre of the circle and take hold of the hand or wrist of another person. This is then repeated with the other arm. Each person should be holding only one hand with each hand. There should not be a cluster of three together. Once it is established that they are all ready announce that they are in a knot. The task is to untie it without anyone letting go.

If the group is really struggling you can break one link – this should enable a speedier resolution.

Ask the group members what skills they would have needed to make this happen quicker. What skills did the group use to succeed? What have these skills got to do with anger management?

(d) Physiological signs of anger

Ask for one volunteer to stand next to a new drawing of the anger thermometer. Mark a line at the bottom. Ask the group to suggest how their colleague would be feeling when the thermometer is low. Draw a line a little higher. Repeat the question. How are they feeling now? In what way will their body be reacting, or showing signs of irritation? Keep repeating this one notch at a time. Encourage the volunteer to demonstrate this – to act out the physical response. Take it as high as possible.

List the key signs – sweating palms, butterflies, rise in heart beat, etc. Suggest to the group that as these are physiological reactions, how might they counter them physically. List these strategies. They might include deep breathing, taking time out, or relaxation exercises. Ask the group if anyone has already used any of these techniques. How useful are they? What would enable the group to use them with greater confidence?

NB: This course does not include relaxation strategies, however they can be useful and would be appropriate to add along side the sessions. Relaxation is a skill that needs practice. Participants should be directed to relevant sources of information and support if requested.

(e) Strategies for Knocks and Wind-ups

Use Appendix 2 as a guide. This can be handed out, read from or used as a model for an overhead. The key phrases to emphasise are:

- 'You can't blame anyone else for a Knock.'
- 'Winding up a Wind-up is dangerous.'
- 'Deflate the Pumping thoughts.'

Explain these and ask for any questions.

DEMONSTRATIONS

Knocks

Ask for two volunteers. Get the group to suggest how one person has 'Knocked' the other. They must role play this with the recipient of the Knock *blaming* the other.

Ask the group what the result of this was. Check that they understand the implications of the key phrase – 'You can't blame anyone else for a Knock'. What are the alternatives to blaming?

Wind-ups

Two volunteers. Get the group to suggest a Wind-up from one person to the other. Avoid the extreme and target the more everyday (even though the group might insist the extreme is the everyday). They must role play this with the recipient responding with a new Wind-up.

Ask the group what the result of this was. Check that they understand the implications of the key phrase – 'Winding up a Wind-up is dangerous'. What are the alternatives to winding up a Wind-up?

The 'You Game'

Ask the group to work in pairs. Ask each pair to role play an argument in which one person is accusing the other of not doing something they were supposed to do (i.e. the washing up). Let the pairs run these for up to one minute.

If your group is unlikely to work comfortably in pairs, take two volunteers to role play the suggested argument in front of the group.

Ask for some feedback as to what types of argument were had and how they developed.

Ask the pairs (or the two volunteers) to repeat their argument, but this time they are not allowed to use the words 'you' or 'your'. Allow this to proceed for a couple of minutes and then again ask for feedback. What were the differences between the two arguments? What does the word 'you' do during a dispute?

The exercise should start a discussion as to how language can act to wind people up without realising it. Certain key phrases are particularly antagonistic. Ask the group what other ways of speaking to others can have similar effects. Get the group to practice other arguments to illustrate these points. For example:

1   An argument with no swearing.

2   An argument where you have to keep your hands in your pockets.

(f) Strategies for pumping thoughts
THE POSTMAN/WOMAN SCENE: PART 1

Return to the postman/woman scene. Recreate the series of images leading to violence but this time see it in slow motion – as slow as the two volunteers can move from image one to the final moment.

PART 2

Explain that it will be run through again, but this time the group can stop it at any time (by shouting 'stop!') and they must suggest what could have been done at that moment to prevent the escalation. It is important to remember that the group leader's co-worker is also a 'group member' and can stop the scene and offer suggestions. This is particularly relevant if the group members do not stop the incident themselves. Check out how applicable the key strategy phrases are to this scene.

PART 3

It is now going to be run through again, but this time with the Pumping thoughts being heard simultaneously. Ask for a volunteer to stand just behind the householder or on a chair to the edge of this character. Their job is to speak out aloud the Pumping thoughts of this individual. It should almost be as if the character had a person over their shoulder goading them into action. If the Pumps were recorded when this scene was first done in Session 1, use these as a guide or script. Run through the scene to the point of violence.

One of the major anger management strategies is 'thought stopping'. Ask the group to comment on how they could stop the Pumping thoughts propelling this scene to a conflict. Ask the character of the householder what it was like to have this person over their shoulder speaking to them. Ask them what they would have liked to have said.

PART 4

Ask for another volunteer. This person is the 'shoulder counsellor' and should either stand behind the other shoulder of the householder or on a chair opposite the thought pumper. Explain that the scene is to be repeated but this time the new volunteer's job is to argue against the Pumping thoughts. They should be countering the arguments or trying to convince the householder not to listen. It is important to emphasise the key phrases here and encourage this person to use them:

- 'It's just a Knock ignore it.'
- 'Beware of winding up the Wind-up', etc.

Once completed, ask the householder what it felt like. Then ask for feedback from the two 'thoughts' and the rest of the group. What was the most effective intervention from the 'shoulder counsellor'? Did the householder actually feel at any time like changing the direction of the scene? Of course it is an excellent point to pick up on if this happened naturally when the scene was being run. Ask the group how the work of the 'shoulder counsellor' could take place without the person being there – how could this be internalised?

Another major anger management strategy, linked to 'thought stopping' mentioned above is the use of 'self-calming statements'. This exercise acts to demonstrate their potential. The objective for the group members is to develop this positive self-talk without relying on the 'shoulder counsellor'.

PART 5

The final run-through, but this time with just the 'self-calming statements'. This time the 'shoulder counsellor' is directly trying to change the direction of the scene without the Pumping thoughts in the way. Repeat if any other group member wants to have a go at this role.

Ask the householder for feedback on how this felt. Then ask for feedback from the whole group. Record the statements or moments in this exercise that the group felt to be the most significant.

EXTRA EXERCISE: 'DEVIL AND ANGEL'

If there is time, ask the householder to sit in a chair and ask two volunteers to stand on either side. One is the provoker and the other is the calmer. Their job is to convince the person in the chair that they were either right or wrong to have finished the scene as they did. Allow this scene to be stopped anytime a group member feels they could add support to the 'calmer' side.

This exercise can act to clarify the exact nature of the two positions, but also to look more clearly at the consequences of certain actions, away from the heat of the moment.

(g) Individual diaries

Hand out a diary sheet to each person and ask him or her to write down a personal incident. Ask them to then add what the Pumping thoughts were and then what the 'shoulder counsellor' could have said.

If there are literacy problems, the co-worker should work with those less comfortable about writing. This exercise can also be done in pairs or in the whole group. In these cases each person would announce the incident, look for support as to what the Pumping thoughts were and finally open up a discussion as to what the 'shoulder counsellor' could have said. The method chosen depends on the groupworkers reading of how secure the group feels in this exercise.

(h) Concluding the session

Check with the group that they have understood the material covered in this session. Again hand out diaries (if they have not already got them) and ask them to write up one incident from the current week or one that happened in the past. Ask them to concentrate particularly on the Pumping thoughts and what statements they might say to themselves to counter them.

3 Deflating the pump! (2)

Session Aims: to strengthen the understanding of the strategies for dealing with Knocks, Wind-ups and Pumps. To examine the consequences of not dealing with them.

Session objectives: at the end of the session, participants will have:

1   Examined incidents in their lives.

2   Explored their Pumps and possible self-calming statements.

3   Practised calming the scenarios of other group members.

4   Examined the consequences of not dealing with Knocks, Wind-ups and Pumps.

THE SESSION
(a) Recap of last week

Very briefly go over the material from last week and check if any group member has any questions.

(b) Introduce the aims and objectives of the session

(c) Warm-up
MENTAL WARM-UP
If you won the lottery…

Ask each person in turn to say what he or she would do if they won a lot of money. Whilst some interesting comments will come up here, the purpose of this exercise is to relax the group and take their minds in an unexpected direction. You do not have to focus on what people say in any detail.

PHYSICAL WARM-UP

Circle and the cross

Ask each person to draw a cross in the air with his or her right hand. They should then put that arm down and be asked to draw a circle in the air with their left leg. The group are then asked to do both at once. This is usually very difficult! The exercise can be adapted to ask the group to draw a cross with one limb and perhaps sign their name with another – and so on.

(d) Diaries

Ask the group if anyone has filled in an incident on the diary sheet. If no-one has, ask the group to take a few moments in the session to fill them in. It is also worth discovering why the group is not completing them – there could be a range of relevant reasons. If filling in during the session, ask them to try to write down an incident that is as recent as possible. As with the previous session, ask them to suggest what the 'shoulder counsellor' would have said.

Ask a volunteer to read out their incident and get the group to comment or give feedback.

(e) Strategy practice

This is a repeat of the series of exercises done on the postman/woman scenes from the previous week.

PART 1

Create the volunteer's story in four images. Try and keep it as simple as possible – if possible, stick to two key characters. See it through in slow motion – as slow as the volunteers can move from image one to the final moment. The person whose story it is can either direct or take the lead role themselves. That role will be called 'the protagonist' for the sake of clarity.

PART 2

Explain that it will be run through again, but this time the group can stop it at any time (by shouting 'stop!') and they must suggest what could have been done at that moment to prevent the escalation. Encourage the group to analyse the incident according to the key strategy phrases – 'Don't wind-up a Wind-up', etc.

PART 3

Run through it again but this time with the Pumping thoughts being heard simultaneously. Ask for a volunteer to stand just behind the person playing the protagonist or on a chair to the edge of this character. Their job as in the previous week is to speak out aloud the Pumping Thoughts of this individual. Run through the scene to the final moment.

Ask the storyteller how accurate these Pumping thoughts were and how they might have stopped these thoughts from pushing them towards the conflict. Ask the group to comment on how they could stop the Pumping thoughts.

PART 4

Ask for another volunteer. This person is the 'shoulder counsellor' and should stand opposite the thought pumper. Explain that the scene is to be repeated, but this time the new volunteer's job is to argue against the Pumping Thoughts. They should be countering the arguments or trying to convince the protagonist not to listen. As before, it is important to emphasise the key phrases here and encourage this person to use them.

Once completed, ask the protagonist what it felt like. Check also with the original storyteller if they are not playing the protagonist themselves. Then ask for feedback from the two 'thoughts' and the rest of the group. What was the most effective intervention from the 'shoulder counsellor'? Did the protagonist at any time actually feel like changing the direction of the scene?

PART 5

The final run-through but this time with just the 'self-calming statements'. This time the 'shoulder counsellor' is trying to change the direction of the scene. Repeat if any other group member wants to have a go at this role. It is particularly relevant for the person whose original story it was to play this role.

Ask the protagonist for feedback on how this felt. Then ask for feedback from the whole group. Record the statements or moments in this exercise the group felt to be the most significant.

EXTRA EXERCISE: 'DEVIL AND ANGEL'

As in session two.

(f) Strategy practice

Repeat the exercise above with another person's story. To not make it too repetitive some stages could be omitted. Try to look at a story that is somewhat different from the first.

Depending on time, this could of course be done more than once.

(g) Meetings

This exercise is to introduce the group quickly to role play before the exercise 'A day in the life'. Split the group into two teams. Ask them to stand facing each other several metres apart. Each person should be opposite a partner. Each person is going to walk towards his/her partner, have a brief 'meeting' and then find a reason for parting. The facilitator gives a topic for each meeting. For example:

1   One of you owes the other £10.

2   One of you has been avoiding the other.

3   One of you sold the other a faulty product.

4   One of you spilt a drink on the other.

5   One of you should have met this person last week but you forgot, etc.

Each person walks forward to their partner, completes the short role play (without necessarily finding a resolution) and then goes back to their place. Each meeting is held in rapid succession. It is worth discussing what comes up here, but the main motivation is to make the group comfortable with creating role plays very quickly.

(h) A day in the life

PART 1

Split the group into two teams. These can be as small as two groups of two. Ask the group to create an imaginary character's 'bad day'. They must show a person who is going somewhere, but they receive a number of Knocks and Wind-ups on the way. The scene should end with a role play of what happened when they reached their destination. There should be a minimum of four moments shown.

PART 2

These scenes are shown. After the first run-through, the scene should be shown again but this time stopped at different moments to access the thoughts and feelings. This is also to check that the observing group members are clear about the Knocks, Wind-ups and possible Pumping thoughts. While it is being watched, a volunteer should stand by the thermometer drawing and mark the scale according to how high they think the protagonist has gone. Do this with both groups.

PART 3

The scenes should be repeated again but this time with a volunteer 'shoulder counsellor'. They should follow the protagonist through the scenes, speaking very closely to them, trying to counter the Pumping Thoughts. Allow different people to try this – even someone in the group whose scene is being used (they could be swapped with another group member for example). You could have different 'shoulder counsellors' coming in and out of individual scenes or different people each taking on a scene. It might be necessary to ask one person to speak at a time so that all voices can be heard. This exercise is to be kept as flexible and interactive as possible. The group should constantly be asked what else could be said to keep this person calm.

PART 4

Tell the group that the end moment is going to be run through again but this time they have to stop it, take the place of the protagonist and act out a way of completing the scene which avoids the escalating conflict. The group should be offered the opportunity to replace the protagonist a number of times, so different possibilities can be tried out or rehearsed. If the group feels that particular interventions are very successful at de-escalating the conflict these should be recorded.

   Note that this end scene should be played as it was in the original and not after the protagonist has been calmed down by the 'shoulder counsellors'.

   As before, it is important to note that facilitators are part of the group and therefore can offer suggestions during this exercise. If the group is missing a key way of dealing with the situation (for example 'walking away'), you should suggest this and ask a volunteer to try it out. Of course the group members can reject your suggestion if they don't think it is possible. All ideas, however, should be tried before they are dismissed.

   All these exercises should then be completed with the other group's story.

(i) Consequences

Ask the group to think of a scene that could take place after the 'bad days' that have been shown. You are looking for only one scene which in some way could be related to both group's scenarios – if there is a difference of opinion, choose the scene suggested that you think will offer the most interesting material for examining the consequences of not dealing with Knocks and Wind-ups. This is not necessarily to be an incident of violence. It could be returning home, arriving at work or getting to the probation group.

   See this scene through once. Repeat it but this time ask the group what they think the thoughts and feelings of those people are (not the protagonist), who are affected by this moment. Repeat it again with the group stopping the action and intervening – entering the scene – on behalf of the protagonist. Their objective is to try to perform the scene without affecting negatively the others present. Emphasise the strategies and repeat until the group are satisfied the behaviour of the protagonist does not negatively impact on others.

One version of this might be a person who returns home at night, and because they have had a 'bad day', they shout constantly at their family members. The exercise would examine the effects of this on the partner, children, etc., and also explore how a person might act so as not to have such a negative impact on those around them.

After each intervention, it is important to ask the group what they thought the person intervening was trying to do. This is, first, to elicit the strategies from the group itself and also to encourage a close watching of the scene. It keeps the observers involved.

(j) Concluding the session

Check with the group that they have understood the material covered in this session. Again, hand out diaries (if they have not already got them) and ask them to write up one incident from the week or one that has happened in the past before the next session. Ask them to concentrate particularly on the strategies they could have used or did use in managing their anger in this situation.

Let the group know that the focus of the next session will change and concentrate more directly on their own violence.

4 Jack!

Session aims: to concentrate on and examine in detail violent incidents in the lives of participants.

Session objectives: at the end of the session participants will have:

1   Discovered which violent situations are most relevant to the whole group.

2   Examined real situations in detail.

3   Examined the triggers to those situations.

THE SESSION

(a) Recap of last week

Very briefly go over the material from last week and check if any group member has any questions. Ask the group to talk through any incidents that they have filled in on their anger diaries. If an incident appears particularly significant or violent, mention that it could be dealt with in detail later in the session.

(b) Introduce the aims and objectives of the session

(c) Warm-ups

MENTAL WARM-UP

Truth and lie

Ask the group members, in turn, to introduce themselves and announce one true and one false piece of information about themselves. They can be flippant or serious. The group can get quite involved in trying to guess which is which. This can be encouraged, but individuals should not be forced to reveal if they do not want to.

PHYSICAL WARM-UP

Continuums

Ask the group to imagine a line – a continuum – that stretches from one corner of the room to the other. Explain that you will make a statement and the group members have to stand on that line, according to how much they agree or disagree with the statement. Designate one end of the line to be 'strongly disagree' and the other to be 'strongly agree'.

Start with a simple statement. For example:

- 'I find it difficult to get up in the morning.'
- 'White bread is nicer that brown.'

Ask individuals to explain why they have put themselves in a particular place. Concentrate at first on those who are furthest apart and according to the exercise are therefore in most disagreement. Develop the discussion with a few contributions before moving on to the next question.

The questions can get more serious and/or you can ask the group to pose the questions themselves.

Ask up to five questions – more-or-less according to how lively the discussions have been.

(d) Violence scenarios

The Knocks, Wind-ups and Pumps sessions have in a sense warmed the group up, but will rarely have dealt with specific moments of violence in detail. Explain to the group that the next two sessions will be dealing directly with violence itself. This session is called 'Jack!' in relation to a jack-in-the-box metaphor. Ask the group why the jack-in-the-box might be a useful idea for an anger management course.

Ask the group to create small still images of moments that would lead to violence in their lives. This can either be done in pairs, threes or as a whole group. If the group has been working well in smaller groups, do it that way; if the group seems more focused when working as a whole, then complete the exercise together.

Look at each image. There should not necessarily be one per person, but anything between three and six depending on the size of the group. Examine these and access the thoughts and feelings of all characters using the 'fist above the head/fist on heart' technique. It is important to let the group interpret the images, before the person whose story it is reveals the exact nature of the incident. The intention is to show that one event can have several meanings. This process should also help to clarify the exact nature of the incident under scrutiny. Give a short title to each scene and record it.

(e) Violent scenario continuums

Remind the group of the continuum line that you created in the room during the warm-up exercise. Designate one end as 'extremely likely' and the other end as 'extremely unlikely'. Mention the title of each image in turn and ask the group to stand on the line, according to how likely it would be for them to respond to this situation with violence. For your own purposes, record these responses by drawing a line on a piece of paper and putting a dot and an individual's initials to indicate where they stood.

Ask each person for some feedback as to why they stood in a particular position. If two people are standing at very different points ask the group why there might be this difference. If you think someone has put themselves in a place which you know is false, challenge them gently on this.

This exercise should give a clear idea of the key trigger situations for this group.

(f) Select a story

Ask for a volunteer to agree to examine their incident in detail. If more than one person volunteers, choose the story that appears most relevant to the whole group.

There are two approaches to continuing this exercise. Exercise (I) is less active and shorter than exercise (II). Choose whichever you feel the group would complete most easily. Exercise (II) should be attempted if you have adequate time and a group that is participating well.

(I) THE STORY SEAT

Ask the volunteer to sit on a chair in front of the group. Explain that the group must now find out as much about the incident as possible by asking this person questions. The person in the story seat can only answer questions that have been asked. Continue the questioning until the incident is clear to everyone. It is important for the questions to be both respectful and challenging. In discovering all aspects of the incident, you do not have to accept everything the person in the seat says. Check for inconsistencies and minimisation. Use the language of Knocks and Wind-ups in the questioning and also ask what strategies were clearly not used. Did the person wind-up a Wind-up or blame someone else for a Knock, for example? Both the group, and the facilitator and co-worker should ask questions.

(II) THE STORYTELLER

'The storyteller' is an 'on your feet' version of the story seat. In this exercise, the volunteer is asked by the facilitator to explain the situation by recreating the incident in front of the group. Again, starting with questions from the facilitator the volunteer *shows* what happened. A dialogue might go something like this:

Volunteer: I was in the pub.

Facilitator: Where were you standing?

Volunteer: By the pool table.

Facilitator: So let's imagine the pool table is here. You were standing right by it?

Volunteer: Yes, and my friend was sitting behind me.

Facilitator: X, do you mind sitting just here as the friend…?

The scene is therefore created both with objects becoming the physical space (chairs etc.) and group members taking on roles. The scene is never acted, as such, only the stage is set. When an incident is recreated in this way, it often becomes apparent that the description does not fit the reality. If the person recalls how they turned round and hit somebody, you might find out that this could not have been possible, because from what the volunteer described, there was a pool table in the way. They must have deliberately walked around the table. Rather than challenging people with the version the facilitator presumes to be true, you can use the evidence before your eyes, to push for a clearer and less sanitised or minimised version.

Constantly check what the person was thinking and feeling throughout this process, and also comment on the Knocks and Wind-ups that occurred. Check too what other people in the scene may have thought, and ask the people in other roles how the incident appeared from where they were sitting or standing. Develop all aspects of the incident right up to the moment of violence.

(g) Finding the triggers

Explain to the group that all violence has some form of trigger. A trigger is something that taps into your emotions or stimulates certain thoughts. Triggers can both stimulate a certain series of Pumping thoughts or can act as a short cut to the emotions. A person may not just have one trigger, but they may experience a series of triggers over time which push them towards violence. In addition, triggers might relate to something that occurs repeatedly, always with the same effect. They are personal and each person's own life history, background and beliefs will generate their own particular set. This section explores this idea so that the group can start to discover what triggers their own violence.

Check that the group understands the significance of the trigger and ask if they can identify what were the triggers for the story just completed. Note that the triggers to violence can occur in rapid succession or they may happen over time. Also triggers can often be hidden. They might relate to the fact that the event is similar to an occurrence in someone's past, to a phrase someone said or a particular way of talking. The people in the incident at hand might have no knowledge of what has triggered the violence.

(I) TRIGGER TABLEAUX

Ask the group to create a still image of each trigger identified. Try to find approximately four images. Ask the group to give a 'trigger title' to each image. What is it that really pushes the person at that moment? Often triggers are described as a personal rule that has been broken. So in a scene where someone comments on another person's family, the trigger statement might be 'No-one insults my family'. Some of these rules might sound innocuous. This exercise is about examining how they become translated into action.

(II) THOUGHTS AND FEELINGS

Using the 'fist above head/fist on heart' technique ask the group to comment on the thoughts and feelings of each character in each tableau. How does this trigger make this person feel? It is important here is to examine how quickly a trigger (which might be a simple comment) can tap into a very powerful emotion. It is thus the person's reaction to and thoughts about the trigger that are the key and not the action of the trigger itself.

The debate here should be widened by asking whether the triggers outlined here as part of one group member's story, are relevant to the others. The purpose of these exercises is to enable group members to understand the concept, so that they discover their own triggers and are aware of how these connect to their own feelings and actions.

(III) RAPID FIRE

Ask the group to return to image one. You are going to see each image in rapid succession. At the clap of your hands, they should change into the next image. With each image, the rest of the group should shout out the title or trigger that accompanies it. Repeat this until you can move quickly from clap one, clap two, clap three to clap four. It should literally go bang, bang, bang, bang. What you want to demonstrate is the physical effect of the trigger in propelling a person to the moment of violence.

Ask the group to comment on this exercise. Ask for feedback on what it means to them. How do triggers affect actions? What are their triggers?

(IV) WHERE DO YOU STAND?

Take the list of title statements or triggers from the previous exercise and ask your co-worker to stand on a chair placed in the middle of the room. Explain to the group that your co-worker is going to make a statement and they have to stand in the room according to their degree of agreement or disagreement. The closer to the chair, the more strongly they agree. Near the walls means that they strongly disagree. It is as if there were concentric circles around the chair. As much as possible, the triggers should be translated into rules – 'It is wrong to do X', 'Nobody has the right to do Y'.

Start by having the questions asked in a straightforward manner. Ask for brief comments on the responses – particularly if you have very different positions in the room. Then start to complicate them. For example, if the opening statement were: 'Nobody insults my family.' You might change this to:

'Nobody insults my family even if my family have acted wrongly.' Or: 'Nobody should talk about my family at all.'

Find the lines of doubt in these rules and the disagreements amongst group members. You want to promote discussion and examine the arbitrary ways in which these rules can be followed. It is important to emphasise how rules and triggers are personal. Even though there might be a lot of agreement about a particular rule, there will still be differences of interpretation and certainly differences in how a person 'reprimands' the individual who breaks it.

An awareness of your personal triggers is a major step to controlling your violence. In acknowledging them, a participant can develop an early warning system to potential moments of danger.

Continue this discussion, trying to cover each statement. You will not necessarily come to a comfortable conclusion. This is only a starting point.

(h) Concluding the session

Check with the group that they have understood the material covered in this session. Again, hand out diaries and ask them to write up one incident from the week or one that has happened in the past before the next session. Ask them to concentrate particularly on the triggers to that situation.

Explain that in Session 5 they will be repeating many of the exercises from Session 4, but on a new person's incident. Ask them to consider if they would like to concentrate particularly on their material.

5 Jack's out!

Session aims: to examine in detail a violent incident and also concentrate on the victim's perspective.

Session objectives: at the end of the session participants will have:

1   Examined another real situation in detail.

2   Examined the triggers to that situation.

3   Examined the effects of violence on a victim.

4   Explored the long-term consequences of violence for a victim.

THE SESSION

(a) Recap of last week

Very briefly go over the material from last week and check if any group member has any questions. Ask the group to talk through any incidents that they have filled in on their anger diaries. If an incident appears particularly significant or violent, mention that it could be dealt with in detail in this session.

(b) Introduce the aims and objectives of the session

(c) Warm-up
MENTAL WARM-UP
Four-minute warning
Ask each group member in turn to say briefly what would they do if the 'end of the world' four-minute warning went off. As before, as much or as little comment as you feel necessary may be given.

PHYSICAL WARM-UP
Push!
Working in pairs, ask each person to put their hands on the shoulders of their partner. Ask them to lean forward and find a balance. Ask them to imagine a line drawn in the sand between them. The aim of this exercise is to push the other person as hard as possible but *neither person* is to cross the line. Let them try it and then ask for feedback. Who succeeded? What is the exercise about? What did you have to do in order to succeed?

This exercise often elicits discussion about balance and equilibrium. Ask your group what the significance of this exercise is to the real world. When do they do this in real life? What would happen if the line in the sand rule were applied to other interactions?

(d) Return to violence scenarios

Repeat the sections in Session 4 from 'select a story' to the end of 'finding the triggers'. Use as different a situation as possible from the previous week. If you can move more rapidly through these sections, you might be able to complete two more stories.

(e) Jack's out!
PART 1
Ask the group to create a tableau of a violent moment. Ideally, it should be one that has either been discussed/used already or represents an incident very similar to areas already touched upon.

Tell the group that the focus of this section is the victim not the perpetrator. The Jack from the jack-in-the-box is out and the incident has happened. Use the 'fist above the head/fist on heart' to access the thoughts and feelings of the victim at that moment. If the group minimise the impact at this stage it is important that your co-worker contributes information, which demonstrates significant impact on the victim. If the group members are struggling, ask them what they would feel if they were in a similar position.

Ask the group to explain the likely damages inflicted on the victim in the tableaux. Explain that people often do not realise the physical damage done. Once a potential list of injuries has been agreed, ask the group to write down on a piece of paper what damage they caused their own victim (ask them to chose one particular incident). If you feel the group are ready for it, ask them to read out what they have written. If anyone has problems with writing, the co-worker should help them complete their contribution. If members of the group choose the most minimal incident, ask them to repeat the exercise with a more serious offence.

PART 2

Ask the group to create three scenes of what happened after the moment represented by the image from Part 1. These can be talking and moving scenes. This can either be done in pairs, in threes or as a whole group. The three scenes should show the consequences of this incident for the victim and should be both short term and long term. Allow the group to play with the time scale – if they want, the scene can be the next day or the following year. Either have each group create a sequence of three or if they are less confident just one scene each.

Watch all the scenes. Develop a debate from each, examining in detail the different long-term and short-term consequences of a violent incident. What were the recurring themes? What were the surprises about what was shown? What was missing?

Often these scenes can be fairly self-explanatory and they require little further exploration. Check with the group, however, to ensure that they have not found anything too upsetting. Allow group members the space to talk about their incidents and how they might differ from what has been shown. Do not be afraid, however, if a scene personally affects an individual. Allow it to be properly discussed and give the person space to see staff privately if necessary.

PART 3

Ask one member of the group who has played a victim in one of the scenes to volunteer to be interviewed as that person. S/he should take a seat in front of the group. The rest of the group now have to ask this person questions about the long-term effects of violence on his/her life. They must do this in a way that shows respect and does not challenge the person playing the role. The volunteer should answer as the victim in the scene s/he completed as much as possible. If s/he is struggling, a member of staff or another group member can offer suggestions as to what might be a likely response.

If a person deliberately tries to sabotage this exercise by minimising or denying the long-term effects, the facilitator should ask another volunteer to give another version of a victim character. It is important that this does not become censorious and a statement of wrong and right. The minimiser should be thanked for their contribution and it should be suggested that this is only one view of a victim and there is perhaps another. If the group really struggles here a co-worker can step in. If you think this might be necessary, it is worth preparing some responses in advance of the session.

Continue the interview until it reaches a natural pause or time runs out. End the exercise by asking each group member to offer one piece of advice to the victim. The last person should be the volunteer playing the victim, who should stand away from the chair and offer their words to the empty chair. This is in order to distance them – derole them – from the character they have been playing. To further derole the person, if you feel they have been particularly absorbed by the character, ask them state how they see themselves to be different from the character they have just been playing.

(f) Concluding the session

Check with the group that they have understood the material covered in this session. Explain that in the next session you are moving to a whole new area and therefore, if they have any questions about any of the material covered during the Jack! sequence they should be asked at this point.

6 The behaviour box (1)

Session aim: to examine in detail the links between violent and other behaviours.

Session objectives: at the end of the session participants will have:

1   Explored the four elements of the behaviour box.

2   Examined the differences between violent behaviour, indirect aggression, 'bottling' behaviour and assertiveness.

3   Examined how each behaviour responds to dilemma situations.

4   Explored the characteristics of people who use each type of behaviour.

THE SESSION

Session preparation

Use insulating/masking tape to create a large cross in the centre of the room, so that the space is divided into four clear square areas. Have access to flip chart paper/wipe board and pens.

(a) *Recap of last week*

Very briefly go over the material from the last session and check if any group member has any questions. The next two sessions will cover new material and therefore it is important to ensure that the group is happy to move on.

(b) *Introduce the aims and objectives of the session*

(c) *Warm-up*

MENTAL WARM-UP

Aliens

Aliens have landed and taken all your memories but you are allowed to keep one – what would it be? Go round the group and ask each person to describe his/her memory. As previously, talk about people's responses, but it is not necessary to spend too long on the exercise.

PHYSICAL WARM-UP

Hypnosis

Ask the group to stand up and get into pairs. Ask them to label themselves A and B. A should then place the palm of their hand very close to, but not touching the nose of B. A is now allowed to move gently wherever they like, but B must keep their nose the same distance from A's palm at all times. Try to get the As to do this slowly at first and smoothly at all times. They should, however, challenge their partner to move into more and more difficult positions.

Swap over. Now B leads A. Once both A and B have been the leader and lead, ask the group which they preferred doing. Take feedback in some detail. How did it feel being lead? Why did you prefer being the leader? Develop the conversation to explore issues of power and control. These are key concerns of Sessions 6 and 7.

(d) The box

Explain to the group that the room is split into four quarters to indicate four different but related types of behaviour. Physically stand in the space as you do this. Ask the group to push their chairs to the edge and stand around each area as you explain briefly what it indicates. The first area is violent or directly aggressive behaviour. The second area is 'indirect aggression', the third is 'bottling behaviour' and the fourth area is 'assertiveness'. Although you can get some feedback on these terms, the group should not worry as the purpose of the session is to explore the concepts in detail.

The rest of this session runs to a set pattern repeated for each box/square. This is:

PART 1: EXPLANATION
PART 2: TABLEAUX
PART 3: DILEMMA
PART 4: CHARACTERISTICS

(e) Jack! or violent behaviour

PART 1: EXPLANATION

Explain again what this area of the box signifies. Emphasise that this whole section is about types of behaviour and not people. Each box represents a type of behaviour. People tend to move between boxes at different times in their lives.

PART 2: TABLEAUX

Ask the group to create an image of somebody using this type of behaviour – direct aggression. Ideally this should be an image of two people. Ask the group to read the image. What's the story? Who are the characters? What has happened? As in all image reading, it is valuable when two people have very different readings or people read an image differently from what the creator originally intended. Access the thoughts and feelings of both characters, using the 'fist above head/fist on heart' technique.

This should be fairly rapid for the group as this will cover very familiar territory.

PART 3: DILEMMA

Ask for two volunteers to role play a small scene. They are to walk into a lift/elevator at the fifth floor at the same time. One wants to descend to the ground and the other wants to go up to the tenth floor. One character is going to use directly aggressive behaviour to get what s/he wants. Explain that any violence is to be performed in slow motion or you should stop the scene at the moment of violence. Once they have decided who is who, ask them to begin.

Ask the group to watch closely and to give feedback on how people using this kind of behaviour respond to difficult situations.

PART 4: CHARACTERISTICS

Continue the discussion above by asking what are the key characteristics of people who use directly aggressive behaviour. Note these down – they will be used as source material for Session 7.

(f) Indirect aggression

PART 1: EXPLANATION

Explain what this area of the box signifies. Indirect aggression is manipulative behaviour that seeks to control others but without using violence. It includes forms of threat and mental violence as well as put-downs and sarcasm.

PART 2: TABLEAUX

Do exactly the same as in the tableaux section under direct aggression. Pay particular attention to the effects of this behaviour on the victim.

PART 3: DILEMMA

Ask for two volunteers to replay the lift/elevator scene, but this time with one person using indirect aggression. Ask the group to watch closely and to give feedback on how people using this behaviour respond to difficult situations. Also explore the key differences between this and direct aggression and how it makes the victim of this behaviour feel.

Ask for the group to volunteer an alternative dilemma and to show how indirect aggression might be used to deal with it. If no-one is prepared to come up with one, suggest the scene of a man and woman (partners) at home: both of them have planned to go out. It is the woman's turn but the man is going to use indirect aggression to get his way. Again, watch the scene and discuss why this behaviour is expressed and what are its effects.

PART 4: CHARACTERISTICS

Continue the discussion above by asking what are the key characteristics of people who use indirect aggression are. Note these down.

(g) Bottling behaviour

PART 1: EXPLANATION

Explain what this area of the box signifies. Bottling behaviour is a passive form of behaviour where a person holds in what s/he really wants and does not portray how s/he is affected by certain incidents. It is a resentful form of passivity. This behaviour is often manifested as indecision and in frequent apology. People 'bottling' can take anger out on themselves or inanimate objects. The extreme end of this box can be self-harm and suicide, and therefore this box needs to be dealt with very sensitively.

PART 2: TABLEAUX

Do exactly the same as in the tableaux section under direct aggression. If the group struggle to come up with their own tableaux you could prepare one. For example, a person sitting withdrawn in a chair with someone leaning towards them trying to speak.

PART 3: DILEMMA

Ask for two volunteers to replay the lift/elevator scene, but this time with one person using bottling behaviour. Ask the group to watch closely and to give feedback on how people who behave in this way respond to difficult situations. Also explore the key differences between this and direct and indirect aggression. Always make sure in the dilemma scenes that the volunteers are using the behaviour which needs to be demonstrated. Check with the rest of the group that the volunteers are doing what has been asked. If someone has got another way of showing a type of behaviour let them replace one volunteer.

PART 4: CHARACTERISTICS

Continue the discussion above by asking what are the key characteristics of people who use bottling behaviour. Note these down.

(h) Assertiveness

PART 1: EXPLANATION

Explain what this area of the box signifies. Assertiveness is a difficult and much misunderstood term. Part of the work in Sessions 6 and 7 is for the group to explore its precise meaning. The first point to emphasise is that it is something that obviously does not belong to the other three boxes. They can thus be used to illustrate non-assertive behaviour. Assertive behaviour is when you are direct, honest and comfortable with expressing your own opinions, whilst accepting the rights of others to express theirs. An assertive person respects others and understands they are responsible for their own life.

PART 2: TABLEAUX

Do exactly the same as in the tableaux section under direct aggression. Pay particular attention to the effects of assertive behaviour. Allow a debate about the context surrounding this tableau, because often whether an image really demonstrates assertiveness depends on what was said, the tone of voice or the relative power of each person in the scene.

PART 3: DILEMMA

Ask for two volunteers to replay the lift/elevator scene, but this time with one person using assertiveness to deal with the dilemma. Ask the group to watch closely and to give feedback on how people using this behaviour respond to difficult situations. Explore the key differences as well between this and direct aggression and how it makes the 'victim' of this behaviour feel.

Keep repeating the scene, allowing different individuals to try out different versions of what might be an assertive response. If one person does something which another group member thinks is not assertiveness, they can shout 'stop': the scene should freeze and they can indicate which behaviour box they think the volunteer was occupying. They should explain which aspect of the demonstration was not assertive and why they think the actions belonged elsewhere. It is important that the group use the other boxes as reference points, as they become a less personalised way of challenging participants' actions.

PART 4: CHARACTERISTICS

Continue the discussion above by asking what the key characteristics of people who use assertiveness are. Note these down.

(i) Concluding the session

Check with the group that they have understood the material covered in this session. Go over the four lists of characteristics and tell the group that these will be the starting point for the next session.

7 The behaviour box (2)

Session aim: to examine the behaviour boxes in more detail and practise using assertive behaviour.

Session objectives: at the end of the session participants will have:

1   Explored whom the four types of behaviour affect.

2   Examined the consequences of violent behaviour, indirect aggression, 'bottling' behaviour and assertiveness.

3   Discussed strategies for mitigating the worst effects of these behaviours.

4   Practised dealing assertively with difficult situations.

THE SESSION
Session preparation

As week 6.

(a) Recap of last week

Very briefly go over the material from the last session and check if any group member has any questions.

(b) Introduce the aims and objectives of the session

(c) Warm-up

MENTAL WARM-UP

Just the ticket!

You have one plane ticket to anywhere in the world. Where would it be to and why? Go round the group and ask each person to say their destination. As previously, talk about people's responses, but do not spend too long on this.

PHYSICAL WARM-UP

Two fingers!

Ask the group to hold their hands up and point their index fingers so the tips touch. With one finger ask them to make a clockwise circle moving away from and then nearer to their body, touching the other index finger on each turn. Ask them to stop this and then repeat with the other finger but this time going anti-clockwise. Finally ask them to do both at the same time. This is difficult but with practice and concentration, it is possible!

(d) Session pattern

As with the previous session, Session 7 runs to a fixed sequence repeated in each of the four box areas. This sequence is as follows:

PART 1: TABLEAU OF CHARACTERISTICS
PART 2: WHO IS AFFECTED?
PART 3: THOUGHTS AND FEELINGS
PART 4: CONSEQUENCES
PART 5: STRATEGIES

(e) Jack behaviour

PART 1: TABLEAU OF CHARACTERISTICS

Ask the group to stand in a circle. Taking the list of characteristics written for Jack behaviour from the last session, ask each group member to choose one. Ask them, on the count of three, to put themselves into a personal tableau of that characteristic. From their positions ask the group to look at each other. Ask them to guess what each person has chosen. Take comments on what the images have in common, and what the key differences are between them.

Ask the group to chose one of their peer's images, which they think best represents this type of behaviour. Always question their decisions to check that the image chosen really fits in the box area – in this case directly aggressive behaviour.

PART 2: WHO IS AFFECTED?

Place the chosen person/tableau at the centre of the direct aggression area. Ask the group to explain whom this type of behaviour affects. Get the group to create tableaux of these people and place them around the first image. You should end up with a group image that you should then ask the group to read. What's the story? What is going on? The people chosen are often very clear characters – friends, family, colleagues etc.

PART 3: THOUGHTS AND FEELINGS

Using the 'fist above the head fist on heart' technique, ask the group what the different characters are thinking and feeling about the behaviour of the person representing the directly aggressive characteristic. In addition, ask them if they could say anything to this person, what would it be? What advice would they give to a person behaving in this way? What do they want from this person?

PART 4: CONSEQUENCES

Ask the group to change the image to what they think would happen to this group of people if the directly aggressive behaviour continues in the future. Ask for this in two stages – the short term and the long term. Get the group to literally change each person/image in turn so that the effects of the behaviour are demonstrated.

Ask the group for feedback on the final image. How are the different people feeling now? Check with the group how this relates to their situation. What are the differences? Where are the similarities?

PART 5: STRATEGIES

Develop this discussion to examine what strategies a person might develop to mitigate the worst consequences of this behaviour. What could they say to the other people in the image? Is it too late once this behaviour has happened? If the person who behaved in a directly aggressive way is left isolated in the final image, what might they do to move forward successfully in the future?

(f) Indirect aggression

Repeat the five parts above in the indirect aggression area.

PART 1: TABLEAU OF CHARACTERISTICS
PART 2: WHO IS AFFECTED?
PART 3: THOUGHTS AND FEELINGS
PART 4: CONSEQUENCES
PART 5: STRATEGIES

(g) Bottling behaviour

Repeat the five parts above in the bottling behaviour area.

PART 1: TABLEAU OF CHARACTERISTICS
PART 2: WHO IS AFFECTED?
PART 3: THOUGHTS AND FEELINGS
PART 4: CONSEQUENCES
PART 5: STRATEGIES

NB: under the bottling behaviour, often the long-term consequences demonstrated can relate to self-harm and suicide. It is important that proper care is taken in covering this section and staff are aware of the institutional or organisational procedures for minimising risk. Any group member who is seen to identify particularly with concerns discussed here should be offered the support required and appropriate staff should be informed of what occurred in the session.

(h) Assertiveness

Repeat the first four parts above in the assertiveness area.

PART 1: TABLEAU OF CHARACTERISTICS
PART 2: WHO IS AFFECTED?
PART 3: THOUGHTS AND FEELINGS
PART 4: CONSEQUENCES

Clearly, the consequences should be positive enough not to require the strategy discussion!

(i) Walking through stories

PART 1: THE WALKING STORY

Ask for a volunteer to tell a story of a conflict or violent incident using the behaviour boxes. They should stand in one box to start telling the story (where they feel they were at the beginning) and explain what happened out loud to the group. They should always be standing in the area that covers the type of behaviour they used at each moment of the incident. So they walk around the box squares marked on the floor. For example, they might start in assertive, move as the story progresses to bottling and then into the direct aggression box.

If another member of the group feels that the person is in the wrong square, they can stop the volunteer and comment on where they think they should be. The staff members can do the same. The storytelling exercise can become a debate with the group, each person stating where they think the protagonist was at a particular moment.

This exercise can be done with a made-up story to start it off. If you feel this might be appropriate, the co-worker could first tell a story following the above guidelines.

PART 2: THE STILL STORY

Choose key moments from the story. These should be moments when the person whose story it was, interacted in a specific way (using direct aggression, indirect aggression or bottling behaviour) with another character. There might be one or several of these moments. These are now going to be role played. Ask for volunteer/s to play the other characters. Give the main volunteer time to explain to his/her peers exactly what happened.

First watch the scenes as they were – in the appropriate behaviour boxes. The actors in the scene should stand in the box according to their behaviour and they should only move boxes if they change their behaviour.

Now they should repeat the scene, but the original storyteller (the protagonist) must act the scene from the assertive box without moving into another. In other words, they should use assertive behaviour in dealing with the incident. As the scene is played out, other group members can shout out if they think the person behaved in a way that belongs to another box. The people playing the other characters should repeat the scene exactly as it was in the original. The key point of this technique is that group members are examining and critiquing the behaviour of a person and not the person him/herself.

Encourage people who shout out to try out the scene themselves. How would they deal with this whilst remaining in the assertive box? As many people as possible should try out each scene. Note on a flip chart the key positive techniques used by group members in the scenes. Lead this into a detailed discussion of what assertiveness is and how it can be practised. One key part that should be emphasised here is that some behaviour that might appear to be 'bottling' behaviour (walking away for example), might in fact be appropriate in some incidences.

To conclude the discussion, ask each group member to say which assertive technique in particular they feel they could use in their life. If valuable, note these down as well.

Of course if you have time the 'walking through stories' section can be repeated with a different volunteer's story.

(i) Concluding the session

Check with the group that they have understood the material covered in this session. Ask the group in particular if they have any questions about the use of the behaviour boxes.

8 Feedback, evaluation and the future

Session aim: to get feedback on the course and make plans for the future.

Session objectives: at the end of the session participants will have:

1   Offered feedback on the exercises and the relevance of the course to their lives.

2   Examined any changes they anticipate in their dealing with dangerous situations in the future.

3   Chosen a personal strategy for the future.

4   Created personal action plans.

THE SESSION

(a) Recap of last week

Very briefly go over the material from the last session and check if any group member has any questions. Explain that this is the final session and therefore it is important that they use the opportunity to ask any remaining questions.

(b) Introduce the aims and objectives of the session

(c) Warm-up

MENTAL WARM-UP

One person

If each participant in the group could meet one person in the world, who would it be? Go round the group and ask each person to give their choice. As in previous mental warm-ups talk about people's responses, but do not spend too long on the exercise.

PHYSICAL WARM-UP

Free choice

Ask the group to choose one of the physical warm-ups done so far in the course. See if you can persuade one group member to run the exercise. Take feedback on how easy or difficult that person found it to explain and run this exercise.

(d) Continuums

Remind the group of the 'violent scenario continuums' that were done in Session 4. These are revisited in the final session. Ask the group to recreate the images of violence that were worked on in this session. Use your own notes to remind the group of these.

After each image is presented, ask the group to stand on a continuum line across the room indicating how likely or unlikely it would be for this type of incident to lead to violence in their lives. Note these down and compare the results to the similar notes made during Session 4. Has anybody moved? If so, in what direction? Show any moves to the group and use them to develop a discussion. Have they really changed? If they have not changed their position, why is this and what would change it?

(e) *Where are you now, and where do you want to be?*

Following on from the discussion above, ask the group to split into pairs and create two still images. One representing where they see themselves now and one representing where they would like to be in the future. Ask the group not to create literal images of where they are (in the room etc!), but something that symbolises where they see themselves in terms of managing their anger.

Read and discuss all the images. After the discussion, ask each pair to prepare two or three images which demonstrate the steps from their original image to the image of their desired future. If they struggle with this, ask them to simply move in three stages between the two images they have already presented.

Ask the group to discuss these stages. What are they? How can they be realised outside the groupwork room? Which stage do you think will be the most difficult and which will be easier?

Ask each group member to write down on the top of a piece of paper where they would like to be in six months' time (in terms of anger management) and then underneath, two or three stages which they need to go through to reach that objective. Each person should be asked to read these out. The co-worker as before should support any individual who has trouble with literacy.

(f) *Favourite strategy*

Again following on from the above discussion, ask the group one at a time to explain which of all the anger management strategies examined during the course they most wish to use in the future. Ask them to describe the strategy, how they would use it and why it is important to them. This can be done in a semi-formal presentational style. Almost as a declaration of intent.

It is important for staff to give feedback at this stage and comment on each group member's choice.

(g) *Feedback*

It is important to get feedback from the group – your customers – on all aspects of the course. This should include:

1   The course learning style – the exercises, images and role plays.

2   The course content – useful to their lives or irrelevant?

3   The contribution of the facilitators – were they a help or a hindrance, clear or confusing?

If you have your own organisational or institutional feedback questionnaires, these should be used.

Valuable feedback information can be gained by making these questions more interactive. Use the continuums or the 'where do you stand?' exercises to develop discussion on all the above areas.

As in Exercise 6 above, it is important to end or incorporate in this section your feedback to the group. How, as staff, do you feel they have done? How have they contributed? What have been the highlights and key moments of the course for yourselves?

(h) Evaluation

Feedback is part of the evaluation process and therefore, information collected above should be monitored carefully. However, a full evaluation of the course can only be done with more thorough pre- and post-testing and longer term participant follow-up. This manual does not contain full evaluation guidelines, because these will change according to the organisation/institution requirements.

For evaluation reports from previous Pump! courses, please contact the TIPP Centre.

(i) Concluding the session, concluding the course

Once all the formal discussions and business has been completed, ask the group for one final word of feedback each. Go around the group to hear these.

It is positive to end the whole course with a quick exercise. The 'clap together' or the 'count to ten' exercises from the Blagg! manual are ideal. The following is also a positive and light-hearted way to end.

COUNT TO FIFTY

Standing in a circle, ask the whole group to count to fifty, one at a time. The catch however is that for every nine and ten figure (nineteen, twenty, twenty-nine, thirty etc.) they must not say the number, but instead they say 'boom' for the nine, and 'hiss' for the ten. The counting goes around the circle until fifty (a 'hiss') is reached with no mistakes.

Appendices

1. MODEL DIARY

Questions	Responses
What happened?	
Where were the Knocks?	
Where were the Wind-ups?	
What were the Pumping thoughts?	
What did you feel at the time?	

2. KNOCKS, WIND-UPS AND PUMPS GUIDE
Definitions
A KNOCK

Knocks are given facts that cannot be changed, happen to all people and are not done maliciously. If I go out and it starts to pour with rain and I get annoyed then this is a Knock. I get a bill, the TV set blows up. These are Knocks. They are facts of life. They are not intentional acts of provocation.

A WIND-UP

A Wind-up is a deliberate act. It can be an attitude someone has, it can be a provocative action or comment, or it can be a taunt or threat. The intention is to wind you up. A Wind-up can be combined with a Knock. A response to another's Wind-up will always be interpreted as a Wind-up itself.

PUMPS

A Pump is an internal thought that pushes you up the anger thermometer. It is a thought that pumps you up in response to an external incident – usually a Knock or a Wind-up. Pumping thoughts are the personal interpretation and justification of events that promote and stimulate your anger and sometimes violence.

Strategies
A KNOCK

You cannot blame anyone for a Knock. When a Knock happens, therefore, you have the following options:
- accept it
- ignore it
- laugh it off
- deal with it
- and more.

A WIND-UP

Winding up a Wind-up is dangerous. When a wind-up happens, therefore, you have the following options:
- ignore it
- laugh it off
- deal with it assertively
- and more.

PUMPS

A Pumping thought needs to be deflated, therefore if possible:
- take time out/relax
- calm yourself down
- breathe deeply
- stop the thoughts.

References

Andrews, D.A. and Bonta, J. (1994) *The Psychology of Criminal Conduct*. Cincinnati OH: Anderson.

Bidinotto, R. J. (1994) 'Must our prisons be resorts?' *Reader's Digest*, November, 65–71.

Boal, A. (1979) *Theatre of the Oppressed*. London: Pluto.

Boal, A. (1992) *Games for Actors and Non-Actors*. London: Routledge.

Boal, A. (1995) *Rainbow of Desire*. London: Routledge.

Boal, A. (1998) *Legislative Theatre*. London: Routledge.

Carlson, M. (1996) *Performance: a Critical Introduction*. London: Routledge.

Chandler, M. (1973) 'Egocentrism and antisocial behaviour: The assessment and training of social perspective taking skills.' *Developmental Psychology 44*, 326–333.

Chapman, T. and Hough, M. (1998) *Evidence Based Practice*. London: HMIP, HMSO.

Cox, M. (ed) (1992) *Shakespeare Comes to Broadmoor: The Actors Come Hither*. London: Jessica Kingsley Publishers.

Freire, P. (1970) *Pedagogy of the Oppressed*. London: Penguin.

Gendreau, P. (1996) 'The Principles of Effective Intervention with Offenders'. In: A.T. Harland (ed) *Choosing Correctional Options that Work*. London: Sage.

Goffman, E. (1959) *The Presentation of Self in Everyday Life*. New York: Doubleday.

Goldfried, M.R. and Davison, G.C. (1979) *Clinical Behavior Therapy*. New York: Holt, Reinhart and Winston.

Goldstein, A. and Glick, B. (1994) *The Pro-Social Gang: Implementing Aggression Replacement Training*. Thousand Oaks, California: Sage.

Gottschalk, R., Davidson, W., Gensheimer, L. and Mayer, J. (1987) 'Community based interventions'. In H. Quay (ed) *Handbook of Juvenile Delinquency*. New York: John Wiley and Sons.

Harland, A.T. (1996) *Choosing Correctional Options that Work*. London: Sage.

Heritage, P. (1998) 'The promise of performance: True love/real love'. In R. Boon and J. Plastow (eds) *Theatre Matters: Performance and Culture on the World Stage*. Cambridge: Cambridge University Press.

Hollin, C.R. (1990) *Cognitive-Behavioural Interventions with Young Offenders*. New York: Pergamon Press.

Howell, J.C., Krisberg, B., Hawkins, J.D. and Wilson, J.J. (eds) (1995) *Serious, Violent and Chronic Juvenile Offenders: A Sourcebook*. London: Sage.

Hughes, J. (1998) 'Resistance and expression: Working with women prisoners and drama'. In J. Thompson (ed) *Prison Theatre: Perspectives and Practices*. London: Jessica Kingsley Publishers.

Jones, P. (1996) *Drama as Therapy: Theatre as Living*. London: Routledge.

Johnstone, K. (1985) *Impro*. London: Methuen.

Kohlberg, L. (1976) 'Moral Stages and moralisation: The cognitive-developmental approach'. In T. Lickona (ed) *Moral Development and Behaviour: Theory, Research and Social Issues*. New York: Holt, Rinehart and Winston.

Lipsey, M. (1989) 'The efficacy of intervention for juvenile delinquency: Results from 400 studies.' Paper presented at the 41st annual meeting of the American Society of Criminology.

Lipsey, M. (1992) 'Juvenile delinquency treatment: A meta-analytic inquiry into the variability of effect'. In T. Cook, H. Cooper, D. Cordray, H. Hartmann, L. Hedges, R. Light, T. Louis, and F. Mosteller (eds) *Meta-analysis for Explanation*. New York: Russell Sage.

Martinson, R. (1974) 'What Works? – Questions and answers about prison reform'. *The Public Interest 35*, 22–54.

Martinson, R. (1979) 'New findings, new views: A note of caution on prison reform'. *Hofstra Law Review 7*, 243–258.

McGuire, J. (ed) (1995) *What Works: Reducing Reoffending*. London: Wiley and Sons.

McGuire, J. and Priestley, P. (1985) *Offending Behaviour: Skills and Stratagems for Going Straight*. London: Batsford.

Miller, J. (1996) *Search and Destroy: African-American Males in the Criminal Justice System*. Cambridge: Cambridge University Press.

Moreno, J.L. (1983) *The Theatre of Spontaneity*. New York: Beacon House.

Novaco, R.W. (1975) *Anger Control: The Development and Evaluation of an Experimental Treatment*. Lexington, MA: D.C. Heath.

Palmer, T. (1996) 'Programmatic and nonprogrammatic aspects of successful intervention'. In: A.T. Harland (ed) *Choosing Correctional Options that Work*. London: Sage.

Reinelt, J.G. and Roach, J.R. (1992) *Critical Theory and Performance*. Ann Arbor, MI: The University of Michigan Press.

Rose, S. (1998) *Group Therapy with Troubled Youth: A Cognitive-Behavioural Interactive Approach*. London: Sage.

Ross, R. and Fabiano, E. (1985) *Time to think: A cognitive model of delinquency prevention and offender rehabilitation*. Johnson City, TN: Institute of Social Sciences and Arts.

Schechner, R. (1988) *Performance Theory*. New York: Routledge.

Sheldon, B. (1995) *Cognitive-Behavioural Therapy: Research, Practice and Philosophy*. London: Routledge.

Spolin, V. (1963) *Improvisation for the Theatre*. Illinois: Northwestern University Press.

Thompson, J. (1996) 'Stage fights: Violence, conflict and drama'. In M. Liebmann (ed) *Arts Approaches to Conflict*. London: Jessica Kingsley Publishers.

Thompson, J. (ed) (1998a) *Prison Theatre: Perspectives and Practices*. London: Jessica Kingsley Publishers.

Thompson, J. (1998b) 'Theatre and offender rehabilitation: Lessons from the US'. *Research in Drama Education 3*, 2, 197–210.

White, J. (1998) 'The prisoner's voice.' In J. Thompson (ed) *Prison Theatre: Perspectives and Practices.* London: Jessica Kingsley Publishers.

Williams, J. (1996) *Putting Out the Fire.* Austin, TX: Alternative Learning Center.